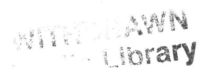

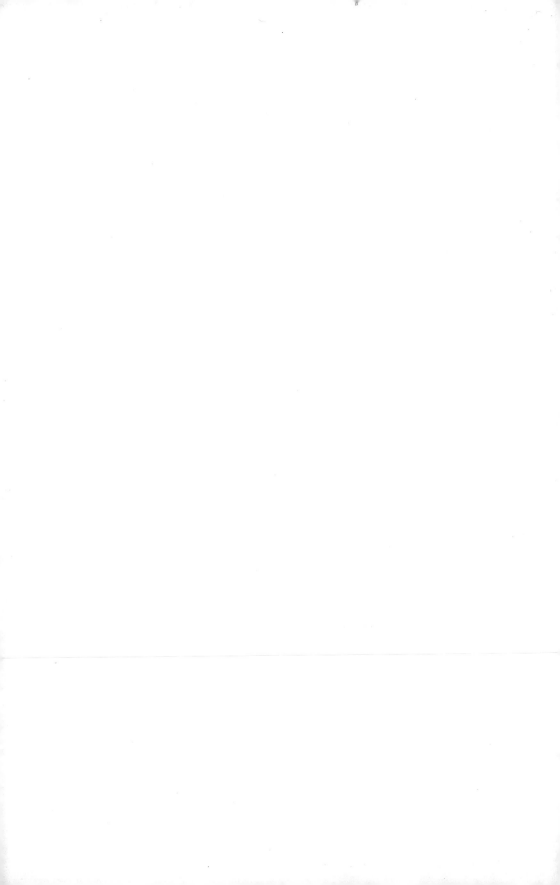

Great Minds of Science

Robert Hooke

Creative Genius, Scientist, Inventor

Mary Gow

Enslow Publishers, Inc.
40 Industrial Road
Box 398
Berkeley Heights, NJ 07922
USA
http://www.enslow.com

Library of Congress Cataloging-in-Publication Data

Gow, Mary
    Robert Hooke : creative genius, scientist, inventor / Mary Gow.— 1st ed.
       p. cm. — (Great minds of science)
    Includes bibliographical references and index.
    ISBN 0-7660-2547-0
    1. Hooke, Robert, 1635–1703—Juvenile literature. 2. Scientists—Great
    Britain—Biography—Juvenile literature. 3. Science—Great Britain—
    History—17th century—Juvenile literature. I. Title. II. Series.
    Q143.H7G69 2006
    509.2—dc22

                    2005031651

Printed in the United States of America

10 9 8 7 6 5 4 3 2 1

To Our Readers:
We have done our best to make sure all Internet addresses in this book were active and appropriate when we went to press. However, the author and the publisher have no control over and assume no liability for the material available on those Internet sites or on other Web sites they may link to. Any comments or suggestions can be sent by e-mail to comments@enslow.com or to the address on the back cover.

Illustration Credits: *Brannon's Picture of the Isle of Wight*, George Brannon, pp. 19, 24; drawing of Robert Hooke copyright © Rachel E. W. Chapman, November 2002, p. 14; Guildhall Library, Corporation of London, pp. 39, 69, 90; Lizzy Hewitt, pp. 30, 45, 86; *Micrographia*, Robert Hooke, pp. 7, 11, 50, 52, 53, 55, 57, 59, 60; Museum of the History of Science, Oxford, pp. 33, 72, 79, 96, 107; National Oceanographic and Atmospheric Administration (NOAA), p. 41.

Cover Illustration: Museum of the History of Science, Oxford (background); drawing of Robert Hooke © Rachel E. W. Chapman, November 2002 (inset).

Contents

"A Person of Great Virtue ..."

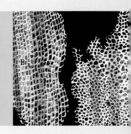

IN 1663, IN ENGLAND, A YOUNG MAN WITH brown hair and a crooked back peered into the eyepiece of a microscope. A relatively new invention, the microscope made small objects appear much larger. This man had modified his microscope to focus light on the specimens he examined. The thin piece of cork he was observing appeared to have tiny holes in it. Wanting a better look at these holes, he removed the cork from under the microscope. He used his pen knife to cut off "an exceedingly thin piece of it."[1] When he placed this sliver of cork beneath the lens, to his delight a new world was revealed.

As he suspected, he could then "plainly perceive it to be all perforated and porous."[2] Thin walls divided the cork into hundreds of little boxes. They were like the compartments in a honeycomb, he remarked. He called them cells, like the small bare rooms occupied by monks in a monastery.

This was the first time Robert Hooke, the young scientist, had ever seen these little boxes. Hooke drew an accurate picture of the cork with its microscopic cells. He wrote a detailed description of his observation. These little boxes accounted for cork's springiness, he said. Curious if the boxes existed in other plants, Hooke looked at other specimens through his microscope. Carrots, ferns, alder wood, burdocks, and reeds, he saw, were also made up of cells.

With these microscopic observations, Robert Hooke had discovered the cellular nature of plants. He had found a system of organization in nature that could not be seen with the unassisted eye. He had also coined the word "cell" to describe these little boxes, a name that would stick. Hooke's discovery of plant cells laid the groundwork for an advance in science that would occur almost two centuries later. In 1839, scientists recognized that cells are the basic units of life and that all living things are composed of cells.

Robert Hooke's description and drawing of cork was one of sixty observations presented in his

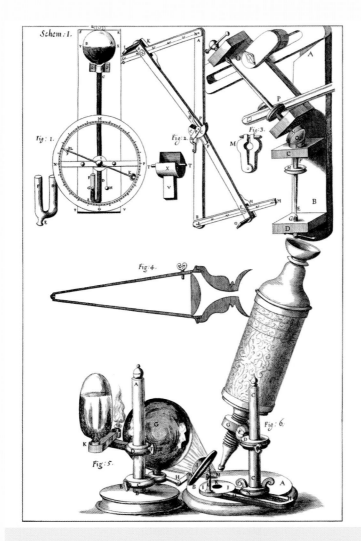

Robert Hooke's microscope as depicted in his 1665 book *Micrographia*. The apparatus to the left of the microscope directed light from a small flame onto the specimens so he could see them more clearly. The instruments at the top of the page include Hooke's wheel barometer and a lens grinding machine that he invented.

book *Micrographia*. Published in London in January 1665, *Micrographia* was a brilliant and astonishing volume. Besides the cork image, it included Hooke's detailed pictures of a bee's barbed stinger, crystals in stone, a housefly's multi-faceted eye, silk threads, and dozens of other subjects as seen through his microscope. His book showed a microscopic world with order and beauty that had never been seen before.

In *Micrographia*, Hooke also described a variety of experiments that he conducted. Some revealed properties of air and light. One showed how a tendril on a wild oat grain changed its shape depending on the level of moisture in the air. He even included a few observations he had done with a telescope.

Scientific Revolution

Hooke lived in a time of enormous strides in understanding the natural world. The period from 1540 to 1700 is often called the "scientific revolution." This revolution began with Nicolaus Copernicus's book suggesting that Earth was a planet revolving around the sun. The earlier, widely held belief was that Earth was at the center of the universe. Knowledge of chemistry, biology, medicine, physics, celestial mechanics, and many other fields expanded enormously during this time. That air had weight, that the heart pumps blood, and that the movement of the planets could be explained by a universal law of gravitation were among the era's discoveries.

Scientists during this time were called "natural philosophers." They sought to learn about the nature of the physical universe. Many of their discoveries came from their new approach to science: finding the causes of natural phenomena through experiments and observations. Today, we take it for granted that scientists conduct experiments and study observations. But this way of learning about the natural world was a new idea in the seventeenth century.

Robert Hooke was one of the greatest experimental scientists of the seventeenth century and possibly of all time. Hooke's career spanned more than forty years. As a young man he was hired to be the first curator of the Royal Society, an English scientific organization. In this position, he was the first professional research scientist in England. From his investigations, Hooke put forth theories about combustion, fossils, and gravity that were confirmed by later scientists. He discovered Hooke's Law of Elasticity. Through his astronomical observations he discovered the red spot on Jupiter and previously unknown stars.

The "scientific revolution" was assisted by the invention and improvement of scientific instruments. Microscopes, telescopes, barometers, and air pumps were among the new devices. It has been said that Robert Hooke improved every important scientific instrument of the seventeenth century.[3] He added sights and precise measuring tools to telescopes, a light source to microscopes, and designed the first air pump in England. Clocks, barometers, and thermometers were improved by Robert Hooke. He invented the universal joint, which is used in the driveshaft of cars and trucks today. He also designed a popular type of window frame.

Along with his scientific achievements, Hooke had other successes. In 1666, the Great Fire of London reduced the heart of the city to smoldering rubble and ash. Robert Hooke had a leading role in London's reconstruction. First, he surveyed the city for rebuilding. Then he turned to architecture. Hooke worked alongside his friend Christopher

Wren, England's most famous architect, designing London landmarks.

With his varied interests and overlapping careers, Hooke led a full and busy life. A diary that he kept for many years shows him dashing about London from demonstrations of scientific experiments, to public lectures, to building site inspections. For business and pleasure he frequented coffee houses to hear news, negotiate contracts, and sip coffee or hot chocolate.

An energetic man, Robert Hooke had suffered from poor health at the beginning of his life. From the time he was sixteen years old he could not fully straighten his back. His spine became twisted and his posture was permanently stooped.

Unfortunately, no portrait of Robert Hooke from his lifetime survives today. Some historians believe that there may once have been a portrait

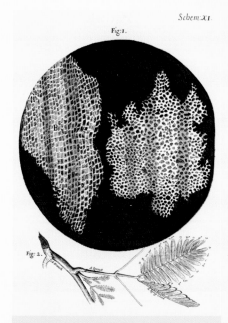

Hooke's representation of cork as seen through his microscope. His Observation XVIII dealt with "the texture of cork and the cells and pores of some other such frothy bodies."

11

of Hooke, but it has since been lost. Others doubt that a portrait was ever painted. Scientific books in the seventeenth century often included an engraved image of the author, but no such portrait was published in Hooke's books. To try to form a picture of this extraordinary man's appearance, historians turn to descriptions of Hooke written by people who knew him.

"He is but of middling stature, something crooked, pale faced, and his face but a little below, but his head is large; his eye full and popping, and not quick; a grey eye," wrote his longtime friend John Aubrey, who wrote short biographies of many of the great men of the seventeenth century. Hooke "has a delicate head of hair, brown, and of an excellent and moist curle [sic] . . . As he is of prodigious inventive head, so is a person of great virtue and goodness,"[4] continued Aubrey.

Richard Waller, who knew Hooke in his later years, wrote that Hooke "was always very pale and lean, and latterly nothing but skin and bone." His eyes, Waller wrote, were "grey and full, with a sharp ingenious look whilst younger." His nose was "thin, of a moderate height and length; his mouth meanly wide, and upper lip thin; his chin sharp, and forehead large." Although he was stooped over, he went "very fast (till his weakness a few years before his death hindered him) having but a light body to carry."[5]

Samuel Pepys (pronounced "peeps") kept a detailed diary of his life in London in the seventeenth century. When Pepys met Hooke, he was impressed by the scientist's brilliance, not his looks. Pepys wrote in 1665, "Mr. Hooke, who is the most, and promises the least, of any man in the world that ever I saw."[6]

Although Hooke's bent figure may have looked unusual, notes in his diary show that he was a fashionable man. He bought fine cloth for his suits, wore a velvet cloak and silk stockings, and frequently had his brown hair trimmed. He owned at least one periwig, a powdered wig popular with men in his time.

Robert Hooke never married, but had a wide circle of friends. Friendships with his school headmaster Richard Busby, early employer Robert Boyle, architect Christopher Wren, and others lasted for decades. Robert Hooke was admired and respected by many distinguished people of his day. Several times he personally met

This drawing of Robert Hooke by Rachel E. W. Chapman was based on descriptions of Robert Hooke's appearance by John Aubrey and Richard Waller.

with King Charles II to demonstrate experiments or show the monarch his inventions.

Competition and controversy often accompanied achievement in the seventeenth century. Robert Hooke had triumphs and successes. He also had disputes. His conflict with the Dutch scientist Christian Huygens, about spring-driven watches, resulted in hard feelings between them. But their competitiveness also improved time-keeping instruments. Robert Hooke engaged in another battle that became legendary. This dispute, about the discovery of the law of universal gravitation, was with Sir Isaac Newton.

2

Island Boyhood

FOR A CURIOUS BOY WITH AN ACTIVE MIND, the Isle of Wight was a spectacular place to live in the seventeenth century. On the south coast were cliffs to climb and curved beaches to explore. High on some cliffs, far above the water, were layers of fossils, the remains of shells and sea creatures that lived millions of years ago.

Across the island, on the north coast, a boy could see the excitement of the 1600s unfold before his eyes. England was entering a new era of global trade and colonization. In the 1630s, sailing ships were carrying settlers to the new Massachusetts Bay Colony and supplies to English settlements in Virginia. Fishing vessels set sail for the bountiful Grand Banks near Newfoundland to catch cod and other fish. Many ships stopped in Wight's sheltered harbors to get fresh drinking water, wheat and barley flour, and other necessities to sustain their crews and passengers on these long ocean voyages.

The Isle of Wight is a diamond-shaped island about twenty-three miles long and thirteen miles wide. It sits just off England's south coast. The island's strategic location and fine harbors account for its great value to mariners in Hooke's time. Beyond its importance for shipping, the Isle of Wight was then and is now an island of extraordinary beauty. With glistening white chalk bluffs, rolling fields, and meandering rivers, the Isle of Wight has long been famous for its magnificent landscape.

Robert Hooke was born on Saturday, July 18, 1635, in Freshwater, a village at the west end of the Isle of Wight. He was the fourth child of Cecily Giles Hooke and the Reverend John Hooke. Robert, the baby of the family, had two sisters, Ann and Katherine, and a brother, John.

The Rev. John Hooke, Robert's father, was not originally from the Isle of Wight. He had moved there in 1610. An educated man, John Hooke may have been a younger son of a landowning, or gentry, family. In that time, oldest sons usually inherited most of their father's wealth. Younger sons had to make their own living. As a member of the clergy, the Rev. Hooke was in a respected career. In 1622, John Hooke married Cecily Giles, a native-born islander.

When Robert was born, the Hookes lived in a two-story cottage in Freshwater. Downstairs, they had a parlor, a study for Reverend Hooke with his desk and books, and a kitchen and pantry. Upstairs, three bedrooms were tucked under the eaves.

Their home was close to All Saints Church, where John Hooke conducted regular religious services. Sometimes he also officiated at another nearby church. He christened babies, including his son Robert.[1] He married local couples and led funeral services for parishioners.

Although Robert Hooke was born more than 350 years ago, we still have some glimpses of his childhood. In his last years, he jotted down a few notes that he intended to use in an autobiography. He did not finish this project, but his notes were used in the brief *Life of Robert Hooke*, written by his friend Richard Waller. Over the years, Hooke had also shared some details of his childhood with others, including the writer John Aubrey. A few stories about Hooke's youth are recounted in one of Aubrey's books.

Hooke's childhood home was in the town of Freshwater on the Isle of Wight. Freshwater Bay with its spectacular cliffs and chalk formations was nearby. This engraving was in a nineteenth century book about the scenery of the island

Robert was not a robust child. A weak and sickly baby, he seemed unlikely to survive, and "for at least seven years his parents had very little hopes for his life."[2] His sisters and brother had been cared for by nurses away from the Hookes' home, a common practice in those days. But because of Robert's frailty, he was kept at home. His digestion was especially delicate. Meat did not agree with him at all and he lived mostly on milk and fruit. Eventually, although he was not strong physically, he became "very sprightly and active in Running, Leaping, etc."[3]

Robert's education began at home. Tutored by his father, he mastered grammar at a young age. He was quick to learn, but when studying he was troubled by persistent headaches. Years later, Robert Hooke wore spectacles, so poor eyesight may have contributed to his boyhood discomfort. Whether Robert eventually attended the Newport School, near his home on the Isle of Wight, is unknown.

Robert Hooke's talent for making instruments showed itself during his early years. As a boy, he made mechanical toys. He discovered that he could imitate and even improve devices. After seeing a brass clock taken apart, he studied its parts. Then, using only wood, he made a working clock of his own. Another time, he made a detailed model of a sailing ship. His little ship's hull was about three feet long. He equipped it with rigging, pulleys, masts, and sails. As a finishing touch, he added small cannons that he could fire as his boat sailed.[4]

Robert's abilities were obvious to his father. John Hooke had originally expected Robert to follow in his footsteps as a clergyman. But as the boy's talent blossomed, John Hooke considered having Robert apprentice to a tradesman, perhaps as a clockmaker. Boys then worked as apprentices for several years with a master craftsman or other tradesman to learn his business.

The seeds of many of Robert Hooke's adult interests were planted during his island childhood. His familiarity with tilted and folded layers of rock on the Isle of Wight contributed to his ideas about earthquakes.[5] Later, when he wrote about fossils he mentioned seeing them at his island home. Hooke had seen countless ships sail out to sea in his childhood. As an adult he made many instruments for ships, including devices to measure ocean depths. Hooke recognized that precise timekeeping could help sailors determine their position in the open sea. One of his long-term projects was to develop a spring-driven watch that would be reliable on a moving ship.

Civil War

During the years when Robert Hooke was exploring cliffs, watching ships, and making toy boats and clocks, political upheaval was occurring in England. For centuries, England had been ruled by a monarch, a king or queen. The monarch inherited the throne and had almost complete authority. Over the years an advisory group called Parliament became a part of the country's government. The Parliament was made up of wealthy landowners. They were responsible for collecting taxes. While Parliament could make recommendations to the king, there was little recourse if he did not accept their ideas.

Almost from the beginning of his reign, King Charles I and Parliament were at odds. They disagreed about the king's support for wars and his view of religion. In 1642, their differences erupted into a civil war. Both sides raised armies. On one side, King Charles I and his supporters wanted to continue the monarchy as it was. The Parliament side wanted changes in government policies on religion and economics. They sought limits to the monarch's power and wanted more authority for themselves.

The early events of the civil war seemed distant from the Isle of Wight. The island was officially under Parliament's control, but most of the islanders were deeply loyal to their king. John Hooke, Robert's father, was a devoted royalist.

In November 1647, King Charles I went to the Isle of Wight and the island was thrust into the center of the country's conflict. Accompanied by members of his court, the king moved in to Carisbrooke Castle. The islanders were honored to welcome their monarch. The castle's owner, a Parliamentarian, was in a difficult spot. While at first he was hosting the king as his guest, soon he was more of a jailer. He was charged with keeping the king on the island and not allowing him to sail away to France or other lands.

King Charles I, who was normally distant from his subjects, was perhaps closer to the islanders than to other commoners. Local community leaders dined with him. John Hooke, a prominent clergyman, may even have been invited to a royal dinner or reception.

Young Robert Hooke apparently had his own brush with the king's court. An artist named John Hoskins, known for his miniature landscapes, was one of the king's official painters. Hoskins accompanied the monarch to the Isle of Wight. Seeing Hoskins' work inspired twelve-year-old Robert to make art supplies and attempt his own drawings. When Hoskins saw the boy's artwork, he

King Charles I stayed in Carisbrooke Castle (above) beginning in November 1647.

was impressed that someone untrained could draw so well.[6] Reportedly, Hoskins was assisted by a boy during part of his stay on the island. That boy may have been Robert Hooke.

The political positions of the king and Parliament were far apart. Although they attempted to negotiate, they could not agree on a compromise about running the country. The Parliamentarians had greater military force. On October 8, 1648, after almost a year on the Isle of

Wight, King Charles I surrendered. He was taken from the island by the Parliament's army.

Coincidentally, within days of the king's departure, John Hooke was dead. Robert Hooke's notes suggest that his father died from a lingering illness. Profound sadness over the king's defeat may also have had a part in his end.[7] In his will, John Hooke left his son Robert, "forty pounds of lawful English money, the great and best joined chest, and all my books."[8] The thirteen-year-old boy's island childhood was over.

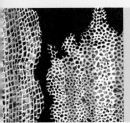

3

Education

WITHIN WEEKS OF HIS FATHER'S DEATH, Robert Hooke was living in London, one of the biggest cities in the world. Details of his move from the Isle of Wight are unknown. Before he died, John Hooke may have made some arrangements for his younger son's future.

London was a bustling city of about 400,000 people. At its heart, inside the medieval defensive wall, houses and shops were crowded together along narrow streets. By Hooke's time, the growing city had spread out beyond the wall and along both sides of the Thames River. Ships that traveled to and from ports in far-off lands tied up at the city docks. At times, it was said, there were so many ships in the river that people could cross the Thames without getting their feet wet.

When he first arrived in London, Robert Hooke had a trial apprenticeship with Peter Lely, a Dutch painter. Lely later became famous for his elegant portraits of English aristocrats. But the smell of the oil paint in the studio gave Robert headaches. Instead of continuing with Lely, the boy turned to academics.

Westminster School

By December 1648, Robert Hooke was a student at one of the finest schools in London. Sons of wealthy and prominent Englishmen studied at the Westminster School. The school was attached to Westminster Abbey, the magnificent church where English monarchs have been crowned since 1066. At Westminster, Robert was not only in a place that offered a superb education, he was also in the care of a farsighted headmaster who recognized his talents.

The exceptional reputation of Westminster headmaster Dr. Richard Busby has lasted more than three centuries. It was said that Busby "had the power of raising what a lad had in him to the utmost height in what nature designed him."[1] Robert Hooke was one of the boys who benefited from this remarkable headmaster's guidance. Busby, like Hooke, was from the Isle of Wight and perhaps a hometown connection brought them together. With his relatively small inheritance, Robert Hooke could not have afforded tuition at the school. The headmaster was known to take in extra students who showed promise. Apparently Robert was one of those boys.

As Robert Hooke settled into school life, an astonishing historic event occurred just a few streets away. Shortly after King Charles I surrendered, a small group of Parliamentarians met. They charged that the king was a traitor. A few days later a special court found King Charles I guilty "as a tyrant, traitor, murderer, and public enemy to the good people" of England. He was sentenced "to death by the severing of his head from his body."[2] On January 30, 1649, the King of England was executed by beheading in front of his palace. At the nearby Westminster School, Richard Busby led his students in prayers for the monarch.

During his years at Westminster, Robert Hooke learned Latin, Greek, Hebrew, and "some other oriental languages,"[3] probably including Arabic. Busby personally tutored him in mathematics, which was not a regular course at the school. In a short time Hooke mastered the first six books of Euclid's Elements, a classical geometry text. At Westminster,

Robert learned to play the organ. He also became intrigued with the possibility of human flight. He designed several flying machines, but eventually reached the conclusion that man's muscles were not strong enough to enable him to fly.

Robert Hooke later commented that his back became twisted when he was sixteen years old. He believed his stoop came from working on a "turn-lathe." A turning lathe is a machine used to shape materials including wood and metal. Robert's comment suggests that he was working as well as studying while he was at school. He may have already started making scientific instruments. Some historians think that it is more likely that Hooke's crooked back was caused by a bone disease than by his labor at the lathe.[4]

Oxford

In 1653, Robert Hooke left London to continue his studies in Oxford, the home of England's oldest university. More than fifteen colleges were educating students there in Hooke's day. Hooke would study at Christ Church, the same college Busby had attended. Busby probably had a role in steering Robert Hooke toward the right people to develop his talents in Oxford. As he started his

Hooke studied at Christ Church, one of the oldest colleges in Oxford. The school is seen across Christ Church Meadow.

studies there, he also began working as an assistant to Dr. Thomas Willis, a friend of Busby's. Willis was a physician who was doing chemistry research.

"About the year 1655," Robert Hooke "began to shew [sic] himself to the world."[5]

In Oxford, the twenty-year-old student was included in meetings of a remarkable group of men who were fascinated by science. Dr. John Wilkins, a charming and admired intellectual, was the head of Wadham College in Oxford. Wilkins was dedicated to the "new philosophy" of science in the seventeenth century. He had equipped a laboratory to conduct scientific experiments. Wilkins hosted weekly meetings of talented men with interest in medicine, chemistry, mechanics, and mathematics. In Wilkins' rooms, they debated scientific topics and investigated a multitude of scientific subjects.

The ideas of two thinkers, Francis Bacon and Rene Descartes, greatly influenced these Oxford scholars. Englishman Francis Bacon believed that by conducting experiments and collecting observations, natural philosophers could discover fundamental laws of nature. His approach was for science to proceed from facts to theory. Frenchman Rene Descartes believed that the physical universe was a complex system governed by mathematical laws. He believed that laws of motion and geometry could explain the material world.

Wilkins' group embraced Bacon's experimental approach to science. They also believed that rational explanations could be found for almost everything in the natural world.[6] Following these beliefs, many of these men in Wilkins' circle made valuable contributions to the advancement of knowledge. Richard Lower performed the first human blood transfusion. Dr. Thomas Willis did groundbreaking research on anatomy and the human brain. John Wallis became one of the leading mathematicians of the day.

Christopher Wren, who became England's most famous architect, was also in Wilkins' group. Wren was skilled in mathematics and astronomy. He assisted with blood transfusion trials and did microscopic observations. Wren and Robert Hooke may have been distant cousins; in Oxford their lifelong friendship began. They both had a wide range of scientific interests. Over many years they cooperated on research, observations, and building projects.

Boyle's Assistant

At Wilkins' invitation, a wealthy, self-taught scientist named Robert Boyle moved to Oxford in 1656 to join their group. Almost immediately, Robert Hooke became his assistant. Boyle was especially interested in chemistry, the science of substances.

In Oxford, Boyle's interest took a turn that would bring him great fame and make his name in the history of science. Robert Boyle had heard

Fr: Diodati   Sculp

ROBERTVS BOYLE NOBILIS ANGLVS MD

Hooke began working as Robert Boyle's assistant in 1656. The airpump designed by Hooke, used for investigations of the properties of air, can be seen behind Boyle, above.

about a pump designed by a German scientist. The device could remove air from a sealed container. Boyle was curious about the properties of air and needed an instrument similar to the German pump for his experiments. When Boyle was unable to get a satisfactory machine from London instrument makers, he asked Hooke for help.

The air pump that Robert Hooke devised was a revolutionary piece of equipment. The "engine," as Boyle and Hooke called it, was a large glass globe resting on a pump. The pump could either pull air from the glass vessel or push air into it. Boyle could set up experiments inside the globe and observe the effects of air on them.

Boyle and Hooke were both extremely curious. They had many ideas for investigations to conduct with the air pump. They dangled a watch in the globe. When they pumped out the air, they could no longer hear the watch ticking. Boyle correctly concluded that air conducts sound. The flame of a burning candle was extinguished after air was pumped from the container. They saw that air was necessary for combustion. Boyle quickly wrote a book of observations of experiments conducted with the air pump. Titled *New Experiments Physico-Mechanical Touching the Spring of the Air*, the book catapulted Boyle to fame in 1660.

Boyle and Hooke continued their studies of air after the book was published. The following year Boyle discovered that there was a relationship between the volume of air and the amount of pressure on it. Boyle's Law is often stated as "the volume of a gas varies inversely with the pressure on the gas." Although the law is named for Boyle, it is widely understood that Hooke made valuable contributions to Boyle's research on this subject. In Boyle's second book about air, he graciously acknowledged Hooke's assistance and gave him credit for his design of the air pump.

Even as Hooke worked with Boyle, he had other interests, too. He was still a student at Christ Church. He would be awarded his master's degree from that college in the early 1660s. Hooke was also conducting experiments using pendulums and magnets. He worked with Wren on microscopic observations. At the same time, he was trying to design a reliable spring-driven watch.

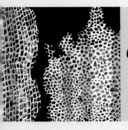

4

"Considerable Experiments"

DURING HOOKE'S OXFORD YEARS, ENGLAND'S government was changing again. After King Charles I's execution, Parliament established a Council of State. Oliver Cromwell, a Parliamentarian and successful military leader, rose to power. The government, however, remained unstable. Cromwell died in 1658. His son succeeded him but was an ineffective leader. In 1660, members of Parliament negotiated an agreement allowing King Charles I's eldest son to return to England. Just eleven years after Charles I was beheaded, King Charles II was welcomed to the throne. The English monarchy was reinstated. The country entered a new era, often called the "Restoration" because the monarchy had been restored.

With King Charles II's return, there was renewed enthusiasm for science in London. Natural philosophers who supported King

Charles I had avoided the city during the Cromwell years. In 1660, the violence of the civil war was past. With the return of the monarchy, people felt the city and country were more stable.

Royal Society

Several of the Oxford group, including John Wilkins, lived in London then. Christopher Wren was Professor of Astronomy at Gresham College there. Robert Boyle still lived in Oxford, but was frequently at the London home of his sister, Lady Ranelagh. Robert Hooke probably accompanied Boyle on some visits. With their love of scientific debate and experiments, members of Wilkins' Oxford group and other natural philosophers met in London from time to time.

The evening of November 28, 1660, was one of those occasions. After Christopher Wren's lecture on astronomy that night, twelve men, including Boyle and Wilkins, got together. They decided to act on an idea that they had considered for some time—to establish a scientific organization. They hoped to initiate "a more regular way of debating things . . . and that they might do something answerable here for the promoting of experimental philosophy."[1]

The organization they founded would soon be known as the Royal Society. Today, more than three centuries later, the Royal Society remains one of the most prestigious science academies in the world. The Royal Society publishes scientific journals, hosts public debates on cutting-edge science, and advises policy-makers in the United Kingdom on scientific matters. The organization promotes excellence in science by recognizing great achievements, funding research, and educating scientists.

The goal of the Royal Society's founders was to advance learning. Boyle, Wilkins and the others believed that experiments were key to discovering truth about the world and the universe. As Henry Oldenburg, the Society's first secretary, explained, "It is our business in the first place to scrutinize the whole of nature and to investigate its activity and powers by means of observations and experiments; and then in course of time to hammer out a more solid philosophy and more ample amenities of civilization."[2]

Although it took time to get business details resolved, the group immediately set to work. One well-connected member contacted King Charles II.

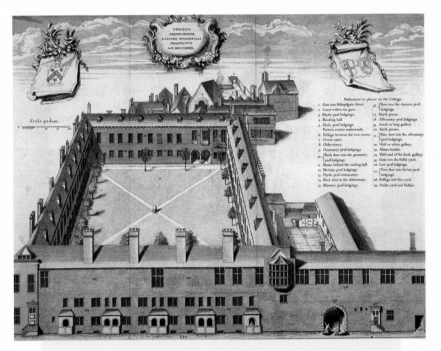

An engraving of Gresham College. Hooke's apartment was in the far right corner of the building.

The king supported their idea for an organization and he agreed to grant them a royal charter. A royal charter would help the society be recognized and respected. The founders hoped that it might also bring them some royal funds. They set out rules stating that new members had to be elected by existing members. Being a scientist was not initially a requirement. Along with natural philosophers, amateur enthusiasts could join the society too.

The First Curator

Boyle, Wilkins, and the others wanted the Royal Society to be an active center of scientific research.[3] They planned to conduct public experiments at weekly meetings. Observing experiments together, the members could discuss what they saw. To describe the person who would lead their weekly investigations, they used a new word, "curator." The job of the curator was supposed to pass from member to member.

Within a few weeks, the Royal Society was meeting every Wednesday afternoon for three hours at Gresham College. Robert Boyle donated his air pump to the group, starting its collection of scientific instruments. On April 10, 1661, Robert Hooke demonstrated the capillary action of water to the group using Boyle's machine. In the coming years, Hooke performed many air pump experiments for the society. He was reportedly the only one who could reliably make the machine work.

The Royal Society's first home was at Gresham College and it remained there for many years. The college was unique. Thomas Gresham, a wealthy businessman, had died in 1579. In his will he left his London mansion and a generous amount of money

A depth sounder and water sampling bottle designed by Hooke. The sounding machine was designed for sailors to measure the ocean's depth in different places. The glass ball and weight, attached to a long string, were dropped off a ship. When the device hit the bottom, the weight fell off the ball. The depth was calculated by measuring the time it took the ball to fall to the bottom and return to the surface.

to found a college. His school did not have enrolled students. Gresham College offered public lectures for the benefit of Londoners. Gresham specified that seven professors would teach and live at the college. They would lecture about religion, rhetoric, music, geometry, astronomy, civil law, and physics.

As the Royal Society settled into the college and a weekly routine, members soon saw that their meetings would be more manageable with one regular curator. In November 1662, Sir Robert Moray proposed that the organization hire someone "to furnish them every day on which they met, with three or four considerable experiments."[4] But, he noted, the curator would not be paid until the society had some money. Hooke was offered the position. Besides the regular experiments, the members required that he also "take care of such others as should be recommended to him by the Society."[5] Hooke accepted the job. As it took nearly two years for the Royal Society to pay him, it seems likely that Robert Boyle supported Hooke in the meantime.

Experiments and Observations

Robert Hooke dove into his Royal Society position as a research scientist. In November 1662 he conducted experiments with small lightweight glass globes. Hooke demonstrated the expansion of gases by heating the globes. As the air inside the globes got hot, the air expanded. Finally, the expanding gas dramatically exploded the fragile globes.

In December, Hooke did more demonstrations with glass globes. This time he set them in water. When the water was cold, the globes floated on its surface. When the water was heated, the globes were less buoyant. They dropped to a lower level in the water. From this demonstration, Hooke made a practical suggestion. He suggested that ships loaded in the cold water of the North Atlantic, might be less buoyant in warmer, tropical water.[6] He recommended that ships traveling from the frigid extremes of northern or southern oceans to the warmer waters of the tropics should carry lighter loads to accommodate this natural change.

In June 1663, Hooke was elected a fellow of the Royal Society. Up to this time, he was the Society's unpaid employee. As a fellow he had equal standing with the organization's other members.

With his curiosity and unquenchable thirst for knowledge, Hooke brought an astonishing range of experiments to the Royal Society. He demonstrated a depth sounder that could help sailors measure deep ocean waters. His device was reinvented in the 1850s and used in laying the first transatlantic telegraph cables.[7] When Wilkins suggested that he keep weather records, Hooke began "A History of the Weather." He began keeping detailed notes about air temperature, humidity, wind direction, air pressure, and other indicators that can help predict weather changes. He also invented the wheel barometer, a compact device for measuring air pressure.

Like many natural philosophers of the time, Hooke was curious about gravity and motion. He conducted experiments to measure the rate of acceleration of objects dropped from great heights. These experiments took him to the highest points in London—the tops of Westminster Abbey and St. Paul's Cathedral. He also tested a pendulum in St. Paul's. (A pendulum is a weight hung on the end of a long string or rod that swings back and forth under the influence of gravity.)

In 1664, Hooke worked on an underwater diving device. First he tried using a series of buckets to supply air to an underwater container.

The home of the Royal Society today.

Then he designed a lead box in which a person could work underwater while breathing through an air pipe that extended above the water's surface.

Hooke continued his interest in astronomy. In May 1664, using a telescope, he discovered the red spot on the planet Jupiter. Watching it move across the planet's face, he determined that Jupiter, like Earth, rotates. Later that year and the following spring, Hooke and Christopher Wren began a series of comet observations. Wren was in Oxford and observed a comet there. Hooke watched from London. At first, both men thought that comets followed straight paths. Their observations, though, indicated that comets' paths were curved. Hooke and Wren both began to correctly suspect that some comets, like planets, orbit the sun.[8]

Shortly after becoming curator, other observations were also occupying Hooke's time. These were seen through a microscope. Royal Society members were amazed by the microscopic world that Hooke showed them.

In 1664, several aspects of Hooke's life came together. The Royal Society was still short of money, but a wealthy businessman named John Cutler made a proposal to Hooke. Cutler offered to pay Hooke an annual salary to deliver public lectures. The Cutler lectures were to address crafts, trades, and mechanical aspects of science. To accompany Cutler's payment, the Royal Society also finally found funds for a small salary for Hooke.

That year, Hooke was invited to live at Gresham College. His rooms were in the corner of the college, next to the Royal Society's space. Along with his parlor, library, and bedroom upstairs, he had storage rooms in the cellar. For his research, he had the Society's laboratory and a platform on the roof for telescopes. Hooke would live at Gresham College for the rest of his life.

Shortly after his move, Hooke had a final bit of good news. In March 1665, he was elected Gresham Professor of Geometry. At thirty years old, he had a home and a career doing what he loved.

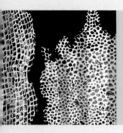

5

Micrographia

LONDONERS HAD NEVER SEEN A FLEA LIKE Hooke's before. They knew about fleas; the little pests were common in England and throughout Europe. About the size of a grain of sand, fleas infested bedding and rugs. They hopped on people, dogs, rats, and other mammals, sucked their blood, and left them scratching the itchy little red welts caused by their bites.

When Robert Hooke looked at a flea through a microscope, he saw something far more exciting than just a speck. "The strength and beauty of this small creature, had it no other relation at all to man, would deserve a description," wrote Hooke in Observation Fifty-three in his book *Micrographia*. The flea's legs, he explained, were long and had joints, "like the foot, leg and thigh of a man." It "springs them all out, and thereby exerts his whole strength at once," he wrote, describing how these tiny limbs gave the flea its amazing ability to leap. He explained how scissor-shaped biters enable this "little busy creature" to "pierce the skin." He admired the flea's beauty, "adorned with a curiously polished suit of sable armor, neatly jointed and beset with multitudes of sharp pins, shaped almost like Porcupine quills."[1]

Besides describing the flea, Hooke drew a large and accurate picture of it. The flea in his book was eighteen inches long. Readers could see the overlapping plates of its external skeleton and its powerful jointed legs. The picture showed an animal with a body suited to its life—protected by a hard shell and capable of jumping to find its food.

"The Most Ingenious Book"

Micrographia was a triumph for Hooke and for the Royal Society. The second book published by the Society, it is one of the most famous volumes in the history of science.

Samuel Pepys, a London gentleman, bought a copy of *Micrographia* in January 1665. He was captivated. "Before I went to bed, I sat up till two o'clock in my chamber, reading of Mr. Hooke's Microscopical Observations, the most ingenious book that ever I read in my life," Pepys wrote in his diary.[2]

49

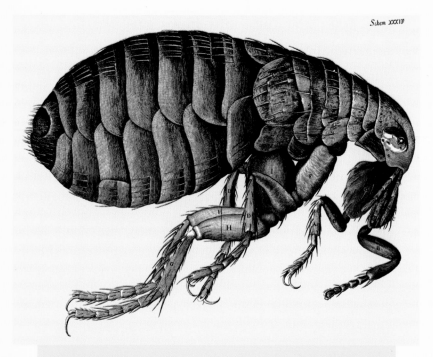
Schem XXXIV

Hooke's drawing of a flea as seen through his microscope.

Micrographia played a vital role in establishing the microscope's value as a scientific instrument. The earliest microscopes were made in the late 1500s, about the same time as the first telescopes. Galileo Galilei, the astronomer, used a microscope in 1609. Telescopes and microscopes were related. Both used glass lenses. In telescopes, the lenses enabled people to see distant objects. In microscopes, the lenses magnified small objects.

Both instruments were improved by Robert Hooke. He added devices for sighting and scales for measuring observations. He also designed mechanical stands to hold the instruments so they could be turned more easily.

The seeds of *Micrographia* were created during Robert Hooke's first years with the Royal Society, when he presented many demonstrations with his microscope. Fascinated, the members asked him to bring at least one microscopic observation to each weekly meeting. This request opened the floodgate of Hooke's creativity.

Beginning in April 1663, every Wednesday, Hooke dazzled the society with his microscope. On April 13, he showed them cork with its hidden structure of cells. That day he also showed them the crystals in a kind of local stone. Tiny worms, mold on leather, the eight eyes of a spider, the head of an ant, and a stunning array of other objects followed.[3] He showed that, through the microscope, the sharp point of a needle was blunt and lumpy and the edge of a razor was rough and irregular.

That June, Hooke was asked to prepare a handsome book of microscopic observations to present to King Charles II. The Royal Society

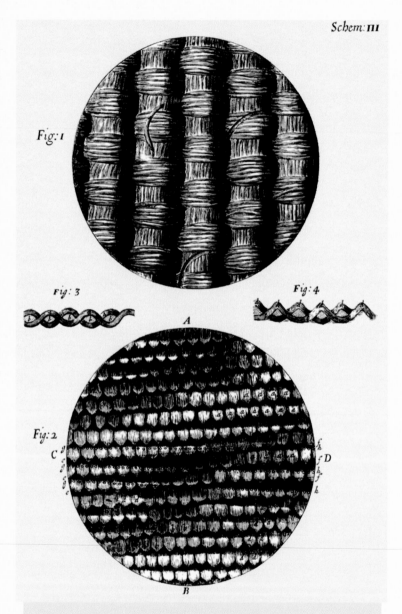

A microscopic view of woven silk fabric. Hooke's fourth and fifth observations in *Micrographia*.

members hoped that the king would come to one of their meetings. Since the monarch had not appeared, Hooke's book could show him their success in advancing knowledge.

Preparing the book, Hooke's artistic talent served him well in his beautiful drawings. The tendrils of blue mold looked like delicate flowers swaying in a garden. His study window was reflected hundreds of times in the minute facets of a fly's eye. Fish scales looked like tiny hand-painted fans.

Hooke's *Micrographia* was a landmark book for several reasons. With its fine illustrations, it showed readers a previously unknown world of complexity and organization in nature. The book also contained discoveries Hooke made and theories he proposed. His explanations of fossilization and combustion were farsighted and accurate. *Micrographia* was also charming and enthusiastic. "Look at this wonderful world," Hooke seemed to say to his readers.

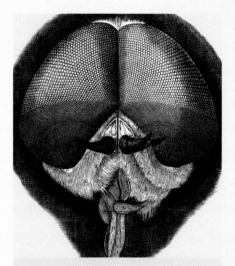

The head of a housefly with light reflected from the hundreds of facets of its eyes.

Micrographia; or, Some physiological descriptions of minute bodies made by magnifying glasses, with observations and inquiries thereupon, was the volume's full title. In its preface, Hooke discussed the limits of mankind's sight, hearing, sense of touch, smell, and even memory. Various instruments, he wrote, let us perceive things beyond our natural limitations. Telescopes revealed stars beyond human sight. Microscopes exposed details invisible to unaided eyes. Thermometers could measure heat or cold more accurately than a person's index finger.

Hooke suggested that in the future even more instruments would be developed. Some of these, he wrote, might transmit sound over great distances or enable man to fly. Hooke would probably have been thrilled that scientific inquiry would eventually lead to space travel, radio telescopes, and electron microscopes.

Hooke's words showed his joy in pursuing and expanding knowledge. "I do not only propose this kind of experimental philosophy as a matter of high rapture and delight of the mind, but even as a material and sensible pleasure . . . so great is the satisfaction of finding out new things," he wrote.[4]

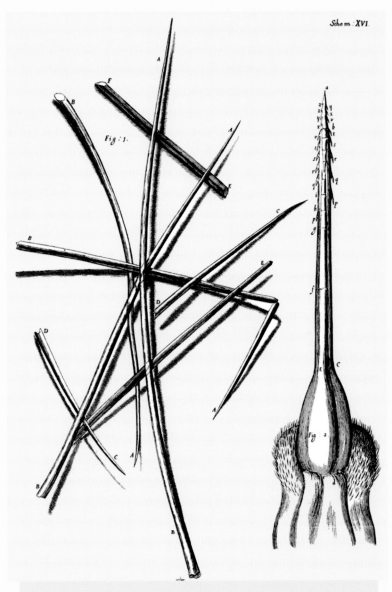

The barbs on a bee's stinger were obvious when Hooke observed it through his microscope

The Observations

The observations in *Micrographia* were organized in order of complexity: from simple, nonliving subjects; to molds and mosses; to plants; to insects, and other tiny living creatures. He concluded with air pump experiments and telescope observations. A sample of Hooke's observations and theories in *Micrographia* follows.

Hooke's sixth observation was "Of fine waled silk or Taffety." He studied a piece of silk ribbon under his microscope. Silk thread is spun from the natural fibers produced by silkworms. Hooke wrote how white silk appeared to be a bundle of clear cylinders. The fibers, he noted, seemed "to be little else than a dried thread of glew [sic]." He remarked that "I have often thought, that probably there might be a way found out to make an artificial glutinous composition, much resembling, if not full as good," as natural silk. He went on to say that he hoped "some ingenious inquisitive person" would pursue the idea.[5] Nylon, a manmade substance now used in clothing and rope, was developed in the 1930s, fulfilling Hooke's prophecy.

In Hooke's ninth observation, he reported on colored rings of light that he observed while

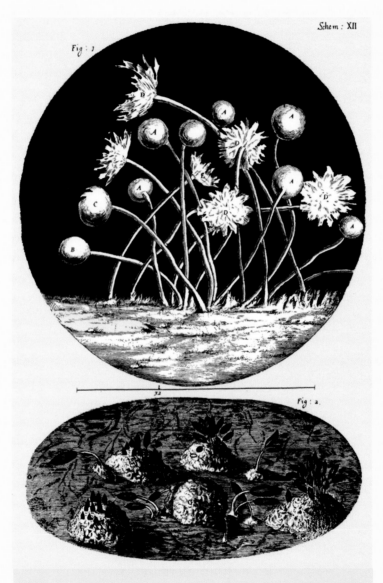

Blue mold growing on a leather book cover looked like a garden under the microscope, above. The lower image shows mildew on a leaf.

examining mica. Mica is a type of mineral that has very thin, almost clear, layers. By moving thin slices of mica Hooke found that he could create different patterns of color. He believed that light was composed of waves. From his observations of the patterns he observed with the mica, he suggested that there must be some property of refraction that causes color. (Refraction is the bending of a ray of light as it passes from one medium to another.) Hooke's ideas about light were insightful. He would return to the subject again.

The sixteenth observation in *Micrographia* dealt with charcoal. In part of the observation, Hooke compared charcoal to wood. He observed that wood, when heated to a high temperature without air, did not burst into flame. Instead, it turned to charcoal. Hooke concluded that there was something in air that created a flame. We now know that a flame requires oxygen, and uses it in a process called oxidation. The element oxygen was not discovered until 1774.

Hooke's ideas about petrified wood were also farsighted. In one observation, he compared petrified wood to newly harvested wood. Both had similar pores or cells. The petrified wood was

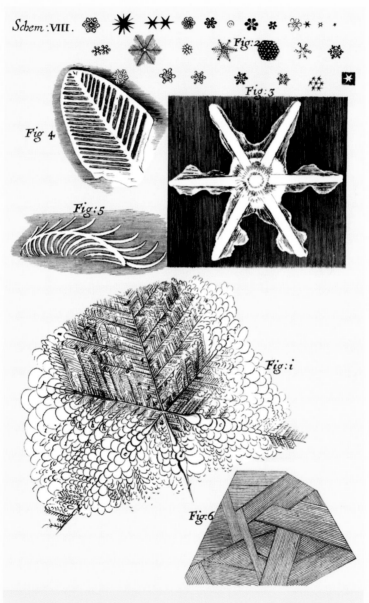

Schem:VIII.

Hooke observed the crystalline structure of snow flakes.

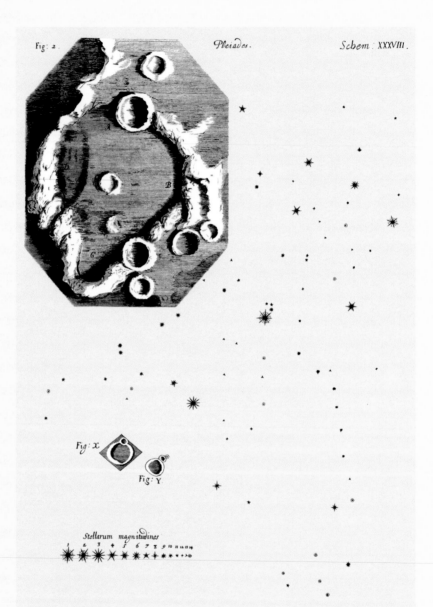

Hooke observed the moon through telescopes and mapped these craters that he observed on its surface.

heavier, harder, darker in color, and did not burn. Hooke suggested that petrified wood was once living. He believed that for a long time, it was soaked with "petrifying water"; rich in "stony and earthy particles." He suggested that those minerals in the water traveled through the wood's pores, gradually "stopping them up."[6] Hooke wrote that this process could happen with wood, other plants, and even animals. Hooke's description of petrification, which is one kind of fossilization, was accurate.

After observing a tendril that grows on an oat grain, Hooke explained how this natural thread could measure humidity—the moisture in the air. The threadlike "beard" of the wild oat grows out of the side of the grain's husk. Extremely sensitive to moisture, the oat beard changes its curve when it gets wet. Observing it under the microscope, Hooke explained that the oat beard was like a little cylinder with channels on its exterior. Exposed to moisture, these channels pulled the thread into a curve. Hooke described how to attach the beard to a needle that could serve as a pointer to measure humidity. An instrument that measures humidity is called a hygrometer.

Micrographia had something for everyone. From the observation of the cellular structure of plants to its huge flea to Hooke's wave theory of light, it was an exciting book. It even included observations of the moon. Having studied lunar craters through a telescope, Hooke wondered what created them. He dropped bullets into soft clay to see if craters were caused by the impact of falling objects. He boiled clay on his stove to see if craters resulted from volcanoes. He ended his book with thoughts about gravity. "To conclude therefore," he wrote, "it being very probable that the moon has a principle of gravitation, it affords an excellent distinguishing instance in the search after the cause of gravitation."[7]

6

London Tragedies

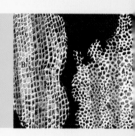

THE SPRING OF 1665 WAS FULL OF PROMISE for Robert Hooke. *Micrographia* was a success. Hooke's salary from the Royal Society was guaranteed. He was delivering the Cutler lectures and he had assumed his position as Professor of Geometry at Gresham College. Countless interesting experiments were waiting to be performed. At the very same time, London was on the brink of two disasters.

The Black Death

In April 1665, one of Hooke's projects was designing horse-drawn carriages. Public coaches were the seventeenth century's buses. They carried paying passengers around London and between towns. In the seventeenth century, more people were traveling around England than ever before and there was great demand for public transportation. Hooke understood springs and the strength of different types of wood. Using this knowledge, he was working to develop safer, more comfortable carriages.[1] As he bounced over London streets testing coaches, Hooke may have seen the first houses to be marked with red crosses.

To the horror of Londoners, in 1665 the dreaded bubonic plague was back. The plague was like a deadly cloud that had hung over Europe since the Middle Ages. Also called the Black Death, the disease killed an estimated 200 million people in Europe in the 1300s. One third of the continent's population died from the plague. After that, the disease was never totally gone. Outbreaks struck towns and cities every few decades.

The bubonic plague is a bacterial disease carried between mammals by fleas. When a flea bites an infected animal, the bacteria enter the flea's system. Bacteria are tiny micro-organisms. The bacteria multiply inside the flea, but do not kill it. When the flea bites a person or another mammal, some of the bacteria are passed to the bitten victim. People infected by the plague suffer chills and fever. Round black spots swell up under their skin. In Hooke's time, most people afflicted by the plague died within a day of the appearance of the spots. Today, the bubonic plague is extremely rare and can be cured with antibiotics.

In the seventeenth century, no one knew that fleas carried this killer. To try to prevent the plague from spreading, sick people were quarantined. Their houses were locked with all family members inside for forty days. A red cross and the words "Lord have mercy on us" were painted on the door. Guards made sure that no one left the house. Often, everyone in a quarantined house died.

The quarantine did not work because rats could move freely between houses. So the plague moved quickly through London. By the summer of 1665, death carts collecting bodies rolled through the city streets. The dead were buried in mass graves beyond the city wall. Two thousand Londoners died of the plague each week that July; six thousand died each week in August.

Almost everyone who could afford to leave London fled. King Charles II and his family moved to Oxford. On June 28, the Royal Society suspended its meetings. Robert Hooke left London with Royal Society members Dr. John Wilkins and Sir William Petty. They packed up a variety of scientific instruments and moved to the country estate of another member. There, they worked on designs for carriages, rigging for ships, and mechanical inventions. Hooke continued his experiments with gravity, measuring the speed at which objects fell when dropped into deep wells.

Winter's cold weather finally slowed the plague and Londoners trickled back to the city. Hooke moved back to his rooms at Gresham College in January 1666. King Charles II and his court returned in February. In March, the Royal Society resumed its weekly meetings. In the year since the first red crosses were painted on London doorways, the plague had killed about 100,000 Londoners— approximately one fifth of the city's population.

Back in London, Hooke was as busy as ever. He was organizing the Royal Society's growing collection of "rarities," unusual items given to or purchased by the group. The early collection included a stuffed crocodile, an armadillo, and an item reported to be a giant's thigh bone. The bone was possibly a dinosaur fossil. Hooke was also setting up the Society's laboratory "which I design to furnish with instruments and engines of all kinds, for making examinations of the nature of bodies, optical, chemical, mechanical, etc."[2] Hooke reported to the Royal Society on observations he made of Mars, experiments with magnets and gravity, and his ideas about the movement of planets. The Royal Society, like all of London, was easing back to normalcy. Then, in early September 1666, disaster struck again.

The Great Fire

Thomas Faryner baked bread for King Charles II. Faryner's bakery stood on Pudding Lane, a narrow street in the heart of London. The center of London, an area of about one square mile, was the oldest part of the city. A medieval defensive wall encircled it. Thousands of homes and shops lined lanes and alleys that twisted through its neighborhoods. Most houses were built of wood. Some had thatched roofs. Print shops, taverns, theaters, laundries, butcher shops, goldsmiths, trade halls, and other businesses crowded together there along with dwellings, schools, hospitals, St. Paul's Cathedral, and dozens of parish churches.

Whether Thomas Faryner failed to fully extinguish his oven fire or some other accident occurred is unknown. In the early hours of Sunday, September 2, 1666, Faryner's bakery was in flames. Fueled by timber buildings and pushed by the wind, the fire spread. It advanced relentlessly, but slowly enough for most people to escape. From Pudding Lane, breezes pushed it south to the docks on the Thames River. The fire rolled west, consuming the city's business center. The Royal Exchange, a kind of seventeenth-century shopping center, burned. Steadily the blaze devoured the city.

All day and night on Monday and Tuesday the fire spread. City courts, shoemakers' shops, coffee-houses, inns, and market stalls burned. Even St. Paul's Cathedral, built of stone but with wooden rafters, was destroyed. The fire was so hot, that the cathedral's lead roof melted and flowed into the streets. Finally, on Wednesday, the wind calmed and firefighting efforts found some success. On Thursday, the city was smoldering, but the fire was contained.

"London was, but is no more,"[3] said John Evelyn, a member of the Royal Society. More than three-quarters of London that was inside the city wall was destroyed. Another sixty-three acres outside the wall were flattened by the blaze. The fire consumed 13,200 houses. Besides St. Paul's Cathedral, eighty-seven churches burned. Markets, docks, and city offices were gone. More than

The Great Fire of London, September 1666, as seen from across the Thames River.

65,000 Londoners were homeless. Amazingly, only nine people reportedly perished in the fire.

Although the blaze had approached Gresham College, the wind had turned it back. Hooke was safe. His rooms and his precious instruments and collections were intact.

London was one of the world's leading cities. King Charles II and city officials knew that they must act quickly. People needed shelter. Businesses needed to resume. At first, the king and city officials considered building a new London. A redesigned city could have wide avenues and open parks, instead of the old jumble of tiny winding streets. A new layout, though, would require thousands of changed property lines. By mid-September it was decided to rebuild London on its old plan, but with wider streets and safer buildings. A rebuilding commission was established in early October. King Charles II appointed Christopher Wren and two others to serve on it. The lord mayor of London appointed Robert Hooke and two others.

The friendship between Wren and Hooke from their Oxford days had continued in London. Wren was a member of the Royal Society. Wren and Hooke liked each other and knew each other's talents. As they embarked on the task of rebuilding London, Hooke answered to the lord mayor and city officials, whereas Wren worked on the king's behalf.

City Surveyor

Hooke laid out London's wider streets and dealt with individual homeowners. He had a sound background in geometry. Instruments he used for astronomy were similar to instruments a surveyor needed to precisely measure angles and slopes. Hooke was skilled in mechanics and engineering.

Wren was already an architect. He had visited Rome and studied classical architecture. In Oxford, he had designed two handsome buildings—the chapel at Pembroke College and the Sheldonian Theater. Wren would design and oversee rebuilding of London's major public buildings, including the Custom House, the Royal Exchange, St. Paul's Cathedral, and dozens of churches.

Robert Hooke played a leading role in writing the Rebuilding Act of 1667. This document spelled out London's new building codes. It limited building heights on the narrowest streets and required that structures have stone or brick exteriors. Traditional thatched roofs were prohibited. (The first thatched roof allowed in London after the Great Fire of 1666 was on the re-created Globe Theater built in 1997. This was only allowed because of the theater's extensive fire protection system.)

One of Hooke's first tasks was resetting London's streets. In March, Hooke was outside on Fleet Street with a staff of laborers. He supervised measurements and saw that wooden stakes marked each road's new wider course. Working at a fast pace, Hooke and the others had almost all of London's roads laid out within nine weeks. Hooke then measured foundations for new buildings and resolved disputes between property owners. He

Christopher Wren, the architect who designed London churches and many public buildings after the fire. His famous St. Paul's Cathedral with its magnificent dome is seen in the background.

certified payments from the city to owners who lost land to the wider streets.

Life at Gresham College changed after the fire. London's city offices had been in the Guildhall, but it was severely damaged in the disaster. Gresham College itself was untouched by the flames. The lord mayor and other officials temporarily moved to the college. Bankers, merchants, and businessmen moved in, too. Traders selling coffee, fabric, furs, cocoa, tobacco, and other imports came to Gresham College to meet buyers and sell their goods. Shops opened in the school's courtyard. Hooke's neighborhood became the center of London as the city was reborn from the ashes.

Hooke was in his early thirties at this time. In spite of his crooked back, he was energetic and active. He liked walking and his stooped figure was a familiar sight as he rushed around London. Working constantly, he was managing two full-time careers. As city surveyor he had the satisfaction of leading the rebuilding effort and he was well paid for his labors. His work for the Royal Society, Gresham College, and delivering the Cutler lectures paid much less but let him pursue his many scientific interests.

Hooke's research continued to be impressive. He delivered a lecture on earthquakes, reported his comet observations, explained why stars appear to twinkle, and modified telescopes to measure observations more accurately. He invented the universal joint, a device that allows a rigid rod to bend in many directions. Hooke used it to make telescopes easier to aim. Sometimes called Hooke's joint, it is used in many machines, including cars and trucks, today.

In one spectacular experiment during this time, Hooke explored the importance of air to the human body. He made a special box from which air could be removed. Hooke himself crouched inside the box and it was sealed. As Royal Society members watched, air was pumped from it. Inside, Hooke felt his ears pop as the air pressure dropped. The experiment could have killed Hooke if the box was truly airtight. Since he did not suffer any permanent injuries, the box probably leaked.

As the 1670s dawned, Hooke added one more career to his full life. Robert Hooke had considerable artistic talent. As Christopher Wren tackled the enormous task of designing so many London churches and public buildings, Hooke began assisting him in his architectural office.

7

Diary Years

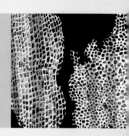

ON SUNDAY, MAY 25, 1673, ROBERT HOOKE had two meetings, including one with the lord mayor of London. He also worked on a catalog of Royal Society books. That afternoon he stopped in at Garaways, one of his favorite coffeehouses. On Monday he met with the lord mayor about mapping London Bridge and nearby docks. He visited a house that had been struck by lightning and saw how the dishes were melted by the blast. That Wednesday, at the Royal Society's weekly meeting, he conducted an "experiment of a damp air which quenched flame." Thursday, he bought books, including one by Galileo about motion. On Friday, he received and read a book about pendulums by the Dutch scientist Christian Huygens. On Wednesday, Thursday, and Friday he also visited Garaways.[1]

We know these details because Robert Hooke began keeping a diary on March 10, 1672. He wrote in it regularly for eight years. His short entries touched on subjects from an elephant he saw at a fair to chemistry experiments. Meetings with builders, bizarre medical treatments, and comments on lenses, compasses, theater productions, and international news were noted. This candid book provides a remarkably personal picture of Hooke and his busy daily life.

With many illustrious friends, Hooke was a social man. He often dined at the homes of Robert Boyle and Christopher Wren. He never married, but his home life was full. Assistants who helped with his experiments sometimes lived in his apartment. A nephew, Tom Giles, worked for him for a couple of years, but died of smallpox in 1677. Hooke's niece Grace, also from the Isle of Wight, lived with him for many years. Hooke was fond of Grace. In his diary he mentioned gowns and jewelry he purchased for her.

Hooke kept detailed notes about finances. Quotes for building projects, payments he received for surveying, the price of lenses for telescopes, and what he paid for wine and cheese were recorded. His expenses show his enthusiasm for books. He purchased classics, including works by Archimedes in Greek and Euclid in Latin. He bought new books about foreign lands, science, and mathematics. His personal library eventually contained more than three thousand volumes.

Several days of almost every week, Hooke visited London coffeehouses. Coffee was a new drink in seventeenth-century London. Imported from Islamic countries, it became phenomenally popular in a short time. Hot chocolate, made from cocoa from South America, was another well-liked new import. Pasqua Rose's, London's first coffeehouse, opened in 1652. By the end of the century there were more than five hundred of these genial establishments in the city. Comfortably furnished with armchairs, tables, and bookcases, they were pleasant places to conduct business, meet friends, and read newspapers.

Hooke mentioned dozens of coffeehouses in his diary, but he was most often at Garaways. Sometimes, he was there twice a day, meeting colleagues and clients about city surveying and architecture or discussing news and ideas with friends and Royal Society members. At times he demonstrated experiments in Garaways' green room. Once he even dissected a porpoise on one of Garaways' tables.

Hooke's diary documents his interests and successes during this period. It shows him refining his spring-driven watches, discovering Hooke's Law, designing scientific instruments, conducting experiments, lecturing, and beginning his distinguished architectural career.

Clocks and Springs

Hooke's interest in timekeeping may have first emerged during his youth on the Isle of Wight, when he saw ships set sail for foreign lands. Sailors faced daunting navigational challenges in the seventeenth century. They did not have reliable tools to know where they were when traveling on the open sea.

Navigators knew how to figure their latitude, the position north or south of the equator, by observing the noontime sun or the North Star when they were in the Northern Hemisphere. But sailors could not compute their longitude, the position east or west, when they were out of sight of land. Hooke and others knew that accurate time-keeping would revolutionize navigation. With an accurate clock, a ship's navigator could measure the exact time that the sun was at its zenith, its highest point in the sky. Comparing that time to

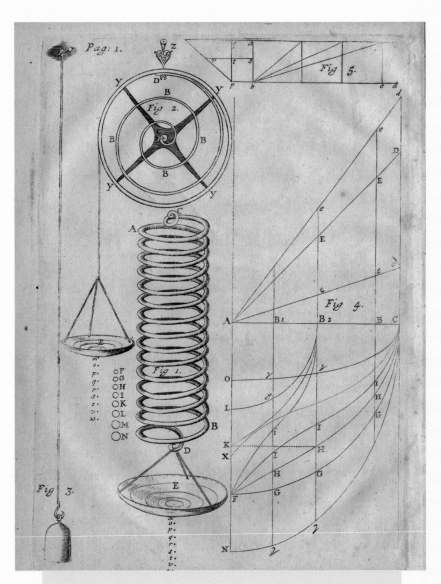

Hooke's springs published in his *De Potentia Restituva*, where he explained Hooke's Law of Elasticity.

when the sun was overhead in a known location like London, a sailor could easily calculate the ship's position east or west of that point.

In the 1660s there were no clocks that were reliable at sea. Older clocks used hanging weights to turn their gears. Some clocks used pendulums that swung back and forth. However, weights and pendulums did not work well in a moving ship tossed by ocean waves. Springs were used in watches, but they were not reliable either. When their springs were tightly wound the watches ran faster than when the springs unwound.

As a young man at Oxford, Hooke designed a spring-driven watch. In the early years of the Royal Society, he demonstrated it at meetings. A clock that was accurate enough to solve the longitude problem could make a fortune for its designer. Hooke considered applying for a patent for his timekeeper. A patent is an official document that gives a person the exclusive right to make or sell an invention. Hooke never applied for a patent on his watch, but he did write to King Charles II about it.[2] He also mentioned his watch in *Micrographia*. But during his busy years after London's fire, Hooke apparently set his timepiece aside.

In early 1675, Hooke was suddenly drawn back to his interest in timekeeping. He heard that Christian Huygens, a Dutch scientist, had developed a pocket watch driven by a spiral spring.[3] Huygens, who lived in the Netherlands, was a member of the Royal Society. Like Hooke, Huygens was interested in scientific instruments. He had made improvements to telescope lenses and had studied the rings of Saturn. Huygens wrote to the Royal Society that his watch operated by a circular pendulum, a spiral spring attached to a balance wheel. The balance wheel regulated the spring's vibration so the watch did not slow down as its spring unwound. Huygens thought that his device had potential for "the discovery of longitude at sea or on land."[4]

Huygens' claim sounded to Hooke like his own watch invention, which he no longer had. When Hooke heard that some Royal Society members were helping Huygens get an English patent, he was alarmed. Hooke had been working with watchmaker Thomas Tompion on other projects involving springs and turned to him. A little diagram accompanies Hooke's diary entry on March 8, 1675. He noted, "Tompion. I [showed] my way of fixing double springs inside of the Balance wheel."[5] Following Hooke's plan, Tompion made a new watch.

On April 7, 1675, Hooke and Tompion met with King Charles II and gave him their timepiece. The king "was most graciously pleased with it and commended it," Hooke wrote, and he "promised me a patent."[6] A month later, they gave the monarch a second watch. This one was gold and was inscribed in Latin:"R. Hook invenit 1658. T. Tompion fecit 1675." (Translations invented by R. Hooke 1658 and made by T. Tompion 1675.)

Huygens was thwarted for the time being. The watch he sent to the Royal Society did not have either a second hand or minute hand. It was also unreliable. Hooke and Tompion kept working on their watches. In August they gave the king a watch that measured seconds and seemed to only gain or lose one minute a day.

As Hooke and Huygens raced to make accurate spring-driven timepieces, they designed balance wheels and anchor-escapements that regulate a spring's movement. These mechanisms improved the performance of watches and are still used today. Springs, however, can be greatly affected by changes in temperature. Temperature change was inevitable on long sea voyages. In the end, neither Hooke nor Huygens applied for a patent. Their watches improved timekeeping, but were not accurate enough to solve the longitude problem. That was not accomplished until English clockmaker John Harrison made a remarkable and reliable chronometer in 1761.

Hooke's Law

In the process of designing watches, Robert Hooke made a discovery that still bears his name. Hooke's Law describes the relationship between the force and stretch of a spring. It is also sometimes called Hooke's Law of Elasticity. Elasticity is the tendency of a body to return to its original shape after it has been stretched or compressed.

Hooke mentioned his discovery of this law in a paper about helioscopes he published in 1675. Helioscopes are telescopes designed for observing the sun. At the end of his paper Hooke included a list of his discoveries that he planned to write about in the future. Hooke wanted to be sure that he could prove that he discovered this natural law even though he was not quite ready to write a detailed paper about it.

Scientists then sometimes protected their discoveries by publishing them as anagrams. The third item on Hooke's list was "The True Theory of Elasticity or Springiness" followed by the letters "cediinoopsssttuu." This anagram was the arrangement in alphabetical order of the letters in the Latin words "Ut pondus sic Tensio." This phrase translates to "the weight is equal to the tension," a summary of his law.[7] Two years later Hooke published a paper explaining his discovery and discussing springs and elasticity in detail.

There are many kinds of springs. A common type is made of coiled wire. Hooke's Law applies to coiled wire springs, to other springs, and to other material with elastic properties. Hooke's Law can also be extended to assess the strength of some building materials, such as steel beams.

To understand Hooke's Law, imagine a simple coiled wire spring. Hooke found that there was a relationship between how much weight was hung from a spring and how much the spring stretched. If a one pound weight was suspended from a six-inch-long coiled wire spring, the spring might stretch to eight inches. When the weight was removed, the spring still returned to its six-inch original length. If a two-pound weight was suspended from the same spring, it stretched farther, but still returned to its original shape when the weight was removed. Hooke found that there was a constant relationship between the weight suspended from the spring and the spring's extension. Unless the spring was stretched too far and its shape distorted, it had a restoring force, or tension, that pulled it back to its original length. Hooke's Law explained that the restoring force of the spring was proportional to the distance the spring was stretched by the weight.

Today, Hooke's Law is often stated as "The power of a spring is in proportion to its extension." Mathematically it is expressed $F = kx$. In this equation F is Force, k is a constant that depends on the stiffness of the spring and x is how far the spring is stretched.

Springs are used in a multitude of everyday machines. They are in bathroom scales, retractable ballpoint pens, garage door openers, trampolines, mousetraps, automobile suspensions, and more. Springs can close doors, make a bicycle ride smoother, and snap the rings of a school binder shut. Using Hooke's Law, designers of these everyday items can determine the right size spring for a job.

The Monument to the Great Fire, designed by Hooke and Wren, is a London landmark. Thousands of people visit the Monument each year, climb its spiral staircase to admire the view and reflect on the fire that devastated London in 1666 and the city's remarkable recovery.

On October 6, 1675, Hooke demonstrated his law to King Charles II. "[Showed] him experiment of Springs. He was very well pleased," Hooke wrote.[8] The king asked him to demonstrate it using a chair. Hooke's diary does not tell whether the king was seated in it or not.

At this same time, Hooke was designing and improving scientific instruments. His helioscopes were valuable for observing sunspots. He designed a Gregorian telescope, a kind of reflecting telescope that uses two mirrors to collect light. He devised a screw for adjusting telescopes that made it possible to more precisely measure angles of observations. He put sighting crosshairs into telescopes so astronomers could note the position of a planet or star exactly as it passed the middle of a telescope's sight. Several of Hooke's instruments were used at the Royal Observatory in Greenwich, England.

Architect

During the 1670s Hooke became one of London's leading architects. As the city continued its recovery from the great fire, Christopher Wren was in charge of a massive amount of work. He was designing office buildings, churches, and the magnificent new St. Paul's Cathedral. Still working as the Royal Society's curator and continuing his city surveying, Hooke began working closely with Wren. Although he was not specifically trained in architecture, Hooke had a fine artistic sense. He also understood the strength of building materials like brick, stone, and timber.

Hooke was soon helping design churches, a city jail, and the Royal College of Physicians. Besides drawing plans, Hooke oversaw construction of buildings. His diary shows that during some weeks he visited building sites every day. He met with stonemasons, reviewed details of foundations, stairways, towers, and gates, and kept an eye on costs.

One impressive project that Hooke and Wren designed together is still standing: the Monument to the Great Fire. Hooke called it "the pillar" in his diary. Started in 1671, the monument was designed and built to commemorate the great fire and to celebrate the rebuilding of London. Exactly 202 feet high, it stands 202 feet from the site of Thomas Faryner's bakery, where the fire began. Inside, a spiral staircase with 311 narrow steps ascends from the street to a viewing platform. Since the building opened in 1676, people who have climbed those steps have been rewarded with breathtaking views of London. At the very top of the column, above the platform, sits an urn holding copper flames to recall those three days in 1666 when London burned.

Besides its commemorative significance, Hooke and Wren intended the monument to be useful to science. Originally, they hoped to use the column as a zenith telescope. They planned to observe stars and comets as they passed directly over it. Unfortunately, the column vibrated too much to get meaningful measurements.

In 1674, Hooke was hired to design Bethlehem Hospital for the mentally ill. With turrets, a clock-tower, and balustrades, Hooke's hospital looked more like a palace than an institution. Tall windows let light pour into the patients' rooms. The hospital's grounds were elegant with gardens and avenues of trees. For all its early glory, the institution's reputation changed over the years with overcrowding and tragic patient care. In the East London dialect, Bethlehem was called Bedlam. Hooke's handsome hospital became the source of the word bedlam, meaning confusion and pandemonium.

Another of Hooke's famous buildings was Montague House, a mansion that stood where the British Museum is today. In his design, Hooke included a new style of window that he had

Bethlehem Hospital, also known as Bedlam, was designed by Robert Hooke in 1675–1676.

devised. Hooke's windows had ropes, pulleys, and weights concealed in their frames. The windows could glide up to open. Because of the ingenious hidden apparatus, the windows would remain open without support from blocks or pegs. Modern sash windows are based on Hooke's design.

Hooke's architectural career lasted for most of the rest of his life. Unfortunately, few of his buildings have survived to the present. But drawings of many of them still exist and they document his impressive talent.

8

The Trouble with Newton

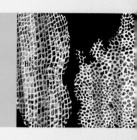

"I HOPE THEREFORE THAT YOU WILL PLEASE to continue your former favours to the Society by communicating what shall occur to you that is philosophical," Robert Hooke wrote in a polite letter to Isaac Newton on November 24, 1679. He told Newton that he would pass on interesting news from the Royal Society. Acknowledging that the two men had past misunderstandings, Hooke wrote, "difference in opinion if such there be . . . me thinks should not be the occasion of Enmity."[1]

Hooke's letter was his first correspondence with Newton in more than three years. Now Secretary of the Royal Society, Hooke was suggesting that it was time to move on from their differences. He even asked for Newton's thoughts on a couple of subjects: elasticity and celestial motion. Isaac Newton was a professor of mathematics at Cambridge University. Seven years younger than

Hooke, Newton would soon be celebrated as one of the greatest scientists of all time.

The paths of Robert Hooke and Isaac Newton first began moving toward each other fourteen years earlier. In 1665 when Hooke's *Micrographia* was published and the plague returned to England, Isaac Newton was a twenty-two-year-old student at Cambridge University. Originally headed toward a degree in law, he had discovered his attraction to natural philosophy. Young Newton was fascinated by optics, the branch of physics that deals with light. He was intrigued by the movements of Earth and other planets around the sun. His genius for mathematics was also emerging.

Soon after the bubonic plague struck London, it reached Cambridge. The university temporarily closed. Newton went home to his family's manor house in Lincolnshire. During the following two years he devoted himself to the study of mathematics, optics, and astronomy. In the quiet countryside, he made advances in all of these fields. When he returned to Cambridge in 1667, Newton was awarded a master's degree and was appointed professor of mathematics.

The Nature of Light

One of Isaac Newton's early scientific interests was the study of light. Newton, like many others, had read *Micrographia*. He was interested in Hooke's remarks about the colored rings he observed through thin pieces of mica.[2] Newton did his own experiments on light using pairs of prisms. Prisms are clear pieces of glass with highly polished surfaces. They are sometimes shaped like pyramids or wedges. Prisms can divide light into a spectrum or rainbow of colors. In his experiments, Newton saw that when white light, like sunshine, passed through one prism, it divided into different colors. When that spectrum passed through a second prism, the light again appeared white. Newton concluded that light was a mixture of rays of different colors. He believed that rays were streams of particles.

In 1671, Newton became a member of the Royal Society. He sent a scientific paper about his prism experiments to the group. In it, he laid out his position that light was a mixed substance that could be divided into its separate color parts. Hooke was asked to review Newton's paper for the Royal Society. He read it but disagreed with

Newton's conclusion. Hooke believed that experiments indicated that light consisted of waves, not particles. (Today, light is understood to have the properties of both waves and particles.) Hooke acknowledged that Newton's prisms showed that the particle theory was a possible answer. But, he asserted, the experiments did not prove that Newton's theory was the only answer. Hooke reported his findings at a Society meeting and sent his comments to Newton.

At first, Newton seemed calm about Hooke's assessment. But a few months later, he wrote a scathing response to Hooke's letter. In it, he belittled Hooke's comments. Newton's harsh letter was published in the Royal Society's journal. Hooke was embarrassed by the public attack on his views.

The tension between them worsened two years later. Newton sent a second paper, "A Hypothesis of Light," to the Royal Society. Some of Newton's observations were similar to Hooke's demonstrations with light and color. Newton heard from a friend that Hooke claimed that most of the paper "was contained in his *Micrographia*."[3] Newton wrote to the Royal Society insulting Hooke's work in *Micrographia*.

A few weeks later, Hooke wrote to Newton. He said that he suspected that Newton had been misinformed about him. Hooke stated that he opposed having public battles and that he valued Newton's ideas. "Your designs and mine I suppose aim both at the same thing which is the discovery of truth," he wrote.[4]

Newton responded politely. He complimented Hooke on his work with colors. He said that Hooke gave him too much credit. "If I have seen further, it is by standing on the shoulders of Giants," Newton wrote.[5] He seemed to be saying that his achievements were built on the work of other great thinkers, including Hooke. The differences between the two men might have ended then if they had not shared additional interests.

Universal Gravitation

Hooke, Newton, and many other thinkers in seventeenth-century Europe wanted to understand and explain the movements of the planets and other heavenly bodies. European natural philosophers knew that Earth and other planets revolved around the sun and that the moon orbited Earth. Through telescopes they had seen moons revolving around Jupiter. Johannes

Kepler, a brilliant German mathematician, had recognized that planets travel in elliptical, not circular, orbits. Kepler's work also showed that planets travel faster when near the sun and slower when they are at greater distances from it. To some thinkers, planetary movement seemed to relate to the phenomenon of gravity, the force that pulls objects toward Earth and gives them weight.

Since his early days with the Royal Society, Hooke had done experiments relating to gravitation and motion. In *Micrographia,* he wrote that he thought that the moon had a "gravitating principle." That would explain its spherical shape and that it "does firmly contain and hold its parts united" as it travels through space.[6] Hooke had investigated gravity and motion by dropping objects down deep wells and from high buildings. With his telescopes, he had observed the movement of the moon, planets, and comets.

Sir Isaac Newton, famous for his laws of motion and universal law of gravitation.

In 1674, Hooke published "An Attempt to Prove the

Motion of the Earth." In it, he put forth three main ideas. The sun attracted the bodies orbiting around it and "all bodies in space possess gravity and an internal attraction within themselves," he wrote.[7] His second assertion was that bodies move in straight lines but can be pulled into orbit around other celestial bodies. His third point was that gravity was more powerful near a body, like Earth or the sun, but weaker farther from it.[8]

As Hooke lectured in London about gravitation and motion, Newton was in Cambridge, pursuing his own studies of the same subjects. Hooke had no way of knowing Newton's considerable progress.

Hooke's friendly letter to Newton in November 1679 unwittingly set the two men on a collision course. In his letter, Hooke mentioned an idea that Newton had not previously examined. Hooke asked for Newton's thoughts "of compounding the celestial motions of the planets of a direct motion by the tangent & an attractive motion towards the centrall [sic] body."[9] In simpler terms, he wondered if planetary orbits could be mathematically described as a combination of a straight-line motion and a pull toward the center of the orbit.

Something similar to the motion that Hooke was describing can be seen with a weight, like a yo-yo, at the end of a string. A yo-yo can be twirled so it stays at the end of its string and revolves around the hand. The hand can be thought of as the sun, the yo-yo as a planet, and the string as gravity. If the hand releases the string, the yo-yo flies out of its orbit, roughly in a straight line, until it falls to the ground.

Prior to receiving Hooke's letter, Newton had been trying to describe planetary motion in terms of centrifugal force.[10] Centrifugal force pulls an object in circular motion outward. Hooke was suggesting that centripetal force might be the key. Centripetal force pulls an object toward the center of its circular motion.

In the months following Hooke's letter, Newton sent him a few polite notes. Hooke, for his part, sent Newton many letters. He wrote about experiments, disagreement with some of Newton's ideas, and other thoughts on celestial motion. In a January 1680 letter, Hooke suggested that gravitational attraction "is always in a duplicate proportion to the distance from the center reciprocal."[11] This was a clumsy way of stating what is now called the inverse square law of gravitation. This mathematical relationship was central to Newton's monumental discovery.

It is unknown whether Hooke, Newton, or someone else first thought of the inverse square law. Newton, however, with his mathematical genius, was the person who explained it best. For years, Newton methodically formulated theories of motion based upon observations, including studies of the velocity and paths of falling objects. Then he rigorously tested his theories against other observations, including the orbits of the moon, Jupiter, and Saturn. He performed extensive calculations and revised his theories when he found they were insufficient.

In the spring of 1686, the Royal Society received the first part of Isaac Newton's extraordinary manuscript *Philosophiae Naturalis Principia Mathematica*. Its Latin title translates into English as "Mathematical Principles of Natural Philosophy." The *Principia*, as it is known, was a truly revolutionary work. In it, Newton presented basic definitions and showed why they could be accepted as true. From those he proved several natural laws. These included three laws of motion and the Universal Law of Gravitation. Taken together, these simple laws explained the clockwork of the universe.

Newton identified gravitation as the force that kept planets in their orbits and pulled objects to Earth. From his calculations and analysis, he showed that every piece of matter in the universe attracts every other piece. He described how the attraction varied according to the mass of the objects and the distance between them. The law was universal because it described a force present at all places at all times.

The Universal Law of Gravitation can be stated this way: Every material particle in the universe attracts every other material particle with a force that is proportional to the product of the masses of the two particles, and inversely proportional to the square of the distance between their centers. The force is directed along a line joining their centers.[12]

Response

Royal Society members were excited about Newton's discoveries. But when the *Principia* was discussed at a Royal Society meeting, Hooke declared that he had stated the inverse square law first. He may have been referring to his January 1680 letter to Newton. Hooke believed that he should be acknowledged in Newton's book. (This type of acknowledgement was and is common. Boyle acknowledged Hooke in *The Spring of the Air*; Hooke acknowledged Wren, John Wilkins, and others in *Micrographia*.) The Royal Society wrote to Newton that they were pleased to publish the *Principia* and mentioned Hooke's response.

"I thank you for what you write concerning Mr Hooke," Newton replied. "I desire that a good understanding may be kept between us."[13] A short time later, Newton's view changed. He wrote an insulting letter about Hooke. Newton complained that Hooke had annoyed him with unwanted suggestions. Newton accused Hooke of being boastful. He wrote that Hooke was incorrect in some of his experiments. Newton ended by saying that Hooke was "a man of strange unsociable temper."[14]

Newton originally had acknowledged Hooke several times in the third part of the *Principia*. Neither Hooke nor other members of the Royal Society had seen this section. In his rage, Newton went through his manuscript and removed almost every mention of Hooke.[15]

The *Principia* was published by the Royal Society and was soon hailed as one of the greatest books of all time. Hooke tried a few times to have his contribution acknowledged, but was unsuccessful.

The two men never reconciled. Newton continued living in Cambridge. Hooke stayed in London with his architectural career and lifelong work with the Royal Society. Newton rarely attended Royal Society meetings while Hooke was alive.

Newton outlived Hooke by twenty-four years. After Hooke's death, Newton was elected President of the Royal Society. In 1705, Newton was knighted by Queen Anne and his genius was celebrated everywhere. Unfortunately, with his fame, and possibly because of his bitterness about their rivalry, Newton's unkind words about Hooke were repeated for centuries. For many years, Hooke was known less for his own outstanding achievements than for his clash with the great Sir Isaac Newton.

9

"Restless Genius"

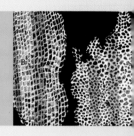

ROBERT HOOKE WAS FIFTY-ONE YEARS OLD when Newton's *Principia* was published. His busy days and many interests continued. In 1686, Hooke returned to a subject that had fascinated him for decades—geology. Geology is the study of the physical nature and history of Earth. Paleontology, the study of fossils, is a branch of geology.

In *Micrographia*, Hooke had written about petrification, a stage in the process of fossilization. In the 1660s, he lectured about fossils and presented his precise drawings of ammonites. Ammonites are extinct shellfish. Hooke discussed these fossils' similarities to living creatures like the chambered nautilus. The general view of fossils in Hooke's time was that they were tricks of nature. Naturally, Hooke disagreed.

In Hooke's lectures he noted that fossils of sea creatures are found in many countries, often far from the ocean. Sometimes they are found in mountains and high above sea level. He recalled that he had personally observed layers of fossils in the cliffs of the Isle of Wight. These layers contained "perfect shells of cockles, periwinkles, muscles, and divers [sic] other sorts of small shell-fishes."[1] He noted that they were usually beneath other layers of rock.

Hooke suggested several propositions to explain fossils. He believed they had been organic matter—plants or animals. From fish and shell fossils he had seen, Hooke suggested that the land and sea may have changed places over very long periods of time. Much of England may have once been underwater and the rise of the land might be explained by earthquakes.

Hooke began a new series of lectures on geology in 1687. In these, he was looking at Earth as a planet. He was trying to understand its shape, surface, and changes. Gravity, he believed, had a key role in the planet's shape and changes. Hooke correctly suggested that Earth is not a perfect sphere, but a flattened sphere that bulges out at the equator. He believed that denser material was at its center, lighter material on its surface, and the atmosphere as its outermost layer. One of his ideas about polar movement was not accurate. However, that theory led him to innovative suggestions that the surface of Earth could be moving—sliding, sinking, and rising.

Considering these movements, Hooke suggested that there had been major changes in Earth's environment. Evidence of earlier times was in fossil layers. Hooke wrote that when regions were below water, they produced "animals or vegetables proper for them, when they came to be dry land and to [lie] above the waters [they produced] animals and vegetables proper and peculiar to that soil element and climate they are furnished with."[2]

Hooke's perceptive view of geology was not immediately accepted. However, his ideas reappear in the work of later scientists who knew of his lectures.[3] Modern geologists are astonished by the accuracy of several of Hooke's propositions.

During the same time that Hooke was teaching geology, he suffered a personal tragedy. His niece, Grace, died in February 1687. Grace, who was twenty-six years old, had lived with Hooke since she was eleven. His diary shows that he was very close to her. His friend Richard Waller wrote that after Grace's death Hooke's sadness "hardly ever wore off."[4]

The following year, Hooke started a new diary. He still visited fashionable coffeehouses. He met frequently with Christopher Wren, Royal Society members, and a new friend, Captain Robert Knox. Knox traveled to India, China, Java, and other distant lands. On one of his travels, he had been held prisoner on Ceylon for several years. Knox shared his stories about exotic places and people with Hooke. From his voyages, Knox brought back curiosities including foreign plants, fish, and pickled peppers to share with Hooke.

Hooke was still working as an architect. He designed the Haberdashers School and Almshouse and several lavish country homes. One commission he enjoyed was serving as surveyor of Westminster Abbey, overseeing repairs and occasional improvements to that magnificent landmark. Hooke's architecture work gave him opportunities to spend time with his old headmaster, Richard Busby. At Busby's request, Hooke designed a small church for the headmaster's hometown. The Willen Church in

Shells and fossils of similar forms discussed by Hooke in his Lectures and Discourses of Earthquakes.

Newport, on the Isle of Wight, is one of the few buildings designed by Hooke that is still standing.

In 1692, Hooke was awarded his doctorate from the Archbishop of Canterbury to honor his great contribution to natural philosophy. It was an award he had earned with a lifetime of achievement. As England's first career research scientist, Hooke had shown that experiments yielded knowledge. By planning, conducting, and recording repeatable investigations he had validated the experimental method. His microscopic observations and clear presentation of them established the microscope as a valuable scientific instrument. *Micrographia* opened the door to a previously unknown world.

Hooke's conviction that good scientific instruments could expand man's knowledge went further than microscopes. He used his mechanical genius to design and improve telescopes, barometers, depth sounders, watches, and more. His wave theory of light, analysis of combustion, and geological conjecture were all farsighted and fit in to later discoveries.

Hooke contributed to the successes of other thinkers of his time, including Boyle's work on the properties of air and Newton's discovery of the universal law of gravitation. Hooke's interest in vibration and springs had led to his own discovery of Hooke's Law of Elasticity. This innovative thinker helped shape the development of science and well deserved the title of Doctor Robert Hooke.

Through the 1690s, even as his health began to fail, Hooke was active with the Royal Society. He served on the society's council almost every year of the decade. His interests and duties were as wide-ranging as ever. When the group was given a live peacock in 1699, Hooke cared for it. A few months later, he lectured about an elephant fossil found in Germany. (It was probably the remains of a wooly mammoth.) As the eighteenth century opened, Hooke's health declined rapidly. On July 10, 1702, he gave his final report to the Royal Society.

Robert Hooke died in his rooms at Gresham College on March 2, 1703. He had been housebound for many months. His funeral was held a few days later at St. Helen's Church. Members of the Royal Society attended. Christopher Wren, Robert Knox, and other friends were there. Hooke's final resting place was in a tomb in St. Helen's.

Although he lived a modest life, Robert Hooke died a wealthy man. A chest in his rooms contained nearly 8,000 pounds (English money) as well as gold, silver, rings, and a diamond. He left telescopes, scales, globes, and magnets. His library of more than three thousand books was extraordinary. In modern currency, his estate was worth at least two million dollars. Hooke had started writing a will but had never completed it. In its absence, a distant relative from the Isle of Wight inherited his money and belongings.

His papers went to Richard Waller, who organized Hooke's lectures and penned "The Life of Dr. Robert Hooke." These were published together by the Royal Society in 1705.

In his biography, Waller praised Hooke's instruments, inventions, and experiments. He commended Hooke's "admirable facility and clearness, in explaining the phenomena of nature . . . his happy talent in adapting theories to the phenomena observed, and contriving easy and plain not pompous and amusing experiments to back and prove those theories." Waller wrote that Hooke, "was of an active, restless, indefatigable genius even almost to the last."[5]

Activities

▶ **Activity One: MAGNIFICATION**

When Robert Hooke's *Micrographia* was published, his pictures showed a previously unknown world of complexity and organization in nature. Few people in seventeenth-century England had ever looked through a microscope. They were amazed to see how objects like the point of a needle and a bit of mold looked when magnified by the microscope's lenses.

Microscopes today are far stronger than those in Hooke's time. Even without a microscope you can see details that we miss with the unassisted eye. You will need:

- A magnifying glass
- A newspaper with color pictures
- A shoe
- A finger
- Pencil and paper

A magnifying glass is a lens. Looking at it you can see that both of its faces are curved. The shape of the lens makes objects seen through it appear larger.

Hold the magnifying glass over the color picture printed on the newspaper. Adjust the glass so the image you see through it is clear to your eye. Looking at the picture, you will see dots of different colors. These are the dots of ink.

With the magnifying glass, look at the sole of the shoe. Depending on where you have been and what the sole is made of you will see different things. You may notice individual particles of dirt or small stones caught in its tread. The texture of the sole may appear lumpier through the magnifying glass than to your unassisted eye.

Finally, take a look at the end of your index finger. With the magnifying glass you can see details of your fingerprint. These will include swirls and little cracks in the skin.

The pictures that Robert Hooke drew of his microscopic observations amazed the readers of his book. Because he so accurately represented what he saw, they felt as if they had looked through the microscope themselves. Looking at your fingerprint through the magnifying glass, try to draw a picture of your fingerprint several times larger than it really is, but with all the details you observed.

▶ **Activity Two: ELASTICITY**

Hooke was fascinated by springs. He used springs in his watches and in his designs for carriages. The natural law that Hooke discovered, known as Hooke's Law, deals with springiness. Hooke's Law can be stated this way: "The power of a spring is in proportion to its extension." To do your own demonstrations of Hooke's Law you will need:

- Pipe cleaners
- Paper clips
- Pens, pencils, and markers

Begin by selecting three pens, pencils, or markers of different diameters. They should be cylinder shaped, not tapered or bulging out in the middle. Take three pipe cleaners. Make a small loop at both ends of each pipe cleaner. Secure each loop with a little twist of the wire. Wind each pipe cleaner around a pen or marker. Make sure your turns are smooth and even. Slide the springs that you made off the writing utensils. Bend the loops so that one extends from the top of each spring and one from the bottom. Attach a paper clip to the bottom of each spring by passing it through the bottom loop.

Your three springs will have different lengths and thicknesses. The fattest one will have the fewest turns in its coil and the thinnest one will have the most turns.

Take another pipe cleaner to use as a hook to hang objects from your springs. Wrap it around a bundle of three or four pens. Make sure that it holds them together. Keep one end of the pipe cleaner free to hook through the paper clip.

Holding the upper loop of a spring, attach your hook and weight to the paper clip. Does the spring extend? Does it stay the same? When you remove the weight, does the spring return to its original shape? Now move the weight to another spring. Does this one extend more or less? Now try a heavier or lighter weight for each spring.

A heavier weight will stretch each spring farther. With careful measurements you could determine the constant relationship between the extension of each spring and the weight.

As you experiment, you will see that if you hang a heavy-enough weight from your spring, it will extend but will not bounce back to its original shape. The weight has exceeded the spring's elasticity.

▶ **Activity Three: LIGHT AND COLOR**

In *Micrographia*, Hooke wrote about rings of colors he observed with thin pieces of mica. Hooke was interested in color and light. He believed that light traveled from its source in vibrations or waves.

Today we know that light is waves of energy. Within visible light, there is a range of waves of different lengths. They are mixed together in white light, like sunlight, but can be divided. You see this spectrum of colors divided in a rainbow or when light passes through a prism.

You can do an easy demonstration to see white light reflected as different colors. You will need:

- Liquid dish soap
- A bowl
- A straw or bubble wand

Mix a couple of tablespoons of dish soap with an equal amount of water. Dip the wand or straw into the liquid and blow bubbles. As you watch the bubbles, you will see different colors.

When the white light from the sun or a light bulb falls on the bubble, the thin film of soap interferes with the rays. Some light is reflected and some passes through the bubble. The colors you see relate to the wavelengths of the different light rays and the thickness of the soap film. As the bubble gets thinner, the reflected colors change.

Chronology

1635—Robert Hooke is born in Freshwater, Isle of Wight, England, on January 25.

1648—Moves to London and apprentices briefly with Dutch painter Peter Lely. Begins studies at Westminster School.

1651—Develops a permanent crookedness in his back.

1653—Begins studies at Christ Church, Oxford University, and works as assistant to Dr. Thomas Willis.

1655—Is included in natural philosophy meetings organized by John Wilkins and begins friendship with Christopher Wren.

1656—Robert Boyle moves to Oxford. Hooke becomes Boyle's assistant.

1662—Receives Master of Arts Degree from Christ Church; is appointed Curator of Experiments at Royal Society.

1663—Is elected member of Royal Society and presents observations with microscope.

1664—Moves to Gresham College.

1665—Is appointed Gresham Professor of Geometry; *Micrographia* is published. Bubonic plague outbreak occurs in London.

1666—After Great Fire of London, is appointed City Surveyor.

1668—Lectures on fossils.

1670—Assists architect Christopher Wren in designing London churches and other public buildings.

1672—Begins diary; engages in a dispute with Isaac Newton over the nature of light.

1674—Designs Bethlehem Hospital; publishes "An Attempt to Prove the Motion of the Earth."

1675—Competes with Christian Huygens over spring-driven watches; publishes "A Description of Helioscopes" with Hooke's Law in anagram.

1677—Publishes Hooke's Law.

1679–1680—Corresponds with Newton about centripetal force, gravitation, and more.

1686—Hooke and Newton disagree over inverse square law.

1687—Lectures on earthquakes and fossils. Grace Hooke dies. Newton's *Principia* is published.

1690—Is appointed Surveyor of Westminster; designs Haberdashers' Almshouse.

1703—Dies in his rooms at Gresham College on March 3.

Chapter Notes

Chapter 1. "A Person of Great Virtue ..."

1. Robert Hooke, *Micrographia* (London: Royal Society, 1665 facsimile edition, New York: 1961), p. 113.

2. Ibid.

3. Richard Westfall, "Hooke, Robert," *Dictionary of Scientific Biography*, ed. Charles Coulston Gillispie (New York: Scribners, 1973), vol. 6, p. 487.

4. John Aubrey, *Brief Lives: A Modern English Version*, edited by Richard Barber (Totowa, New Jersey: Barnes & Noble, 1975), p. 168.

5. R. Waller (ed.), *The Posthumous Works of Robert Hooke* (London: Royal Society, 1705, reprinted with an introduction by R. S. Westfall, London: 1969), pp. xxvi–xxviii.

6. *The Diary of Samuel Pepys*, vol. VI, 1665, transcription edited by Robert Latham and William Matthews (Berkeley: University of California, 1972), pp. 36–37.

Chapter 2. Island Boyhood

1. R. Waller (ed.), *The Posthumous Works of Robert Hooke* (London: Royal Society, 1705, reprinted with an introduction by R. S. Westfall, London: 1969), p. ii.

2. Ibid.

3. Ibid.

4. Ibid.

5. Ellen Tan Drake, *Restless Genius* (New York: Oxford University Press, 1996), pp. 60–61.

6. Ibid., p. 11.

7. Lisa Jardine, *The Curious Life of Robert Hooke* (New York: HarperCollins, 2004), p. 52.

8. Ibid., p. 53.

Chapter 3. **Education**

1. Lisa Jardine, *The Curious Life of Robert Hooke* (New York: HarperCollins, 2004), p. 62.

2. Charles Carlton, *Charles I: The Personal Monarch* (London: Routledge and Kegan Paul, 1983), p. 352.

3. R. Waller (ed.), *The Posthumous Works of Robert Hooke* (London: Royal Society, 1705, reprinted with an introduction by R. S. Westfall, London: 1969), p. iii.

4. Stephen Inwood, *The Forgotten Genius: The Biography of Robert Hooke 1635–1703* (San Francisco: MacAdam/Cage, 2003), p. 10.

5. Waller, p. iii.

6. Lisa Jardine, *The Curious Life of Robert Hooke* (New York: HarperCollins, 2004), p. 79.

Chapter 4. **"Considerable Experiments"**

1. Michael Hunter, *Science and Society in Restoration England* (Cambridge, England: Cambridge University, 1981), p. 35.

2. Ibid., p. 37.

3. Ibid., p. 38.

4. Ellen Tan Drake, *Restless Genius* (New York: Oxford University Press, 1996), p. 17.

5. Allan Chapman, *England's Leonardo: Robert Hooke and the Seventeenth Century Scientific Revolution* (Bristol, England: Institute of Physics, 2005), p. 36.

6. Stephen Inwood, *The Forgotten Genius: The Biography of Robert Hooke 1635–1703* (San Francisco: MacAdam/Cage, 2003), p. 37.

7. Ibid., p. 39.

8. Ibid., pp. 75–76.

Chapter 5. *Micrographia*

1. Robert Hooke, *Micrographia* (London: Royal Society, 1665; facsimile edition, New York: 1961), p. 210.

2. *The Diary of Samuel Pepys*, vol. VI, 1665, transcription edited by Robert Latham and William Matthews (Berkeley: University of California, 1972), p. 18.

3. Hooke, pp. vii-viii.

4. Ibid., preface.

5. Ibid., p. 7.

6. Ibid., p. 109.

7. Ibid., p. 246.

Chapter 6. London Tragedies

1. Stephen Inwood, *The Forgotten Genius: The Biography of Robert Hooke 1635–1703* (San Francisco: MacAdam/Cage, 2003), p. 54.

2. Ibid., p. 80.

3. Ibid., p. 88

Chapter 7. **Diary Years**

1. *Robert Hooke's Diary 1672–1680* (London: Wykeham, 1968), pp. 44–45.

2. Stephen Inwood, *The Forgotten Genius: The Biography of Robert Hooke 1635–1703* (San Francisco: MacAdam/Cage, 2003), p. 34.

3. Ibid., pp. 188–189.

4. Lisa Jardine, *The Curious Life of Robert Hooke* (New York: HarperCollins, 2004), p. 198.

5. *Robert Hooke's Diary*, p. 151.

6. Ibid., p. 157.

7. Allan Chapman, *England's Leonardo: Robert Hooke and the Seventeenth Century Scientific Revolution* (Bristol, England: Institute of Physics, 2005), pp. 174–175.

8. *Robert Hooke's Diary*, p. 185.

Chapter 8. **The Trouble with Newton**

1. Stephen Inwood, *The Forgotten Genius: The Biography of Robert Hooke 1635–1703* (San Francisco: MacAdam/Cage, 2003), p. 273.

2. Ibid., p. 150.

3. Ibid., p. 213.

4. Ibid., p. 215.

5. Ibid., p. 216.

6. Robert Hooke, *Micrographia* (London: Royal Society, 1665; facsimile edition, New York: 1961), p. 246.

7. Allan Chapman, *England's Leonardo: Robert Hooke and the Seventeenth Century Scientific Revolution* (Bristol, England: Institute of Physics, 2005), p. 203.

8. Ibid., p. 204.

9. Inwood, p. 274.

10. Ibid., pp. 274–275

11. Chapman, p. 207.

12. Nathan Spielberg and Bryon Anderson, *Seven Ideas That Shook the Universe* (New York: John Wiley & Sons, 1987), p. 78.

13. Richard S. Westfall, *Never at Rest: A Biography of Isaac Newton* (Cambridge: Cambridge University Press, 1980), p. 446.

14. Ibid., p. 448.

15. Ibid., p. 449.

Chapter 9. "Restless Genius"

1. Ellen Tan Drake, *Restless Genius* (New York: Oxford University Press, 1996), p. 176.

2. Ibid., p. 248.

3. Ibid., p. 3.

4. Michael Hunter and Simon Schaffer, eds., *Robert Hooke: New Studies* (Suffolk, England: Boydell Press, 1989) p. 293–4.

5. R. Waller (ed.), *The Posthumous Works of Robert Hooke* (London: Royal Society, 1705, reprinted with an introduction by R. S. Westfall, London: 1969), pp. xxvii–xxviii.

Glossary

architect—A person who designs buildings and supervises their construction.

bacteria—Certain one-celled microorganisms.

barometer—An instrument for measuring atmospheric pressure.

bubonic plague—A contagious disease caused by bacteria carried by fleas.

celestial mechanics—The branch of astronomy dealing with the motion of the planets and other heavenly bodies.

combustion—The process of burning.

commission—A group of people officially appointed to perform specific duties.

cork—The outer bark of a tree, the cork oak.

curator—The person who cares for a museum or collection.

dissect—To cut apart carefully in order to study the parts.

elasticity—Stretchiness, springiness. The ability of a material to return to its original shape after being stretched.

experiment—A controlled investigation to test a theory or demonstrate a fact.

fossil—The remains or impression of a plant or animal in rock.

gravitation—The force of attraction between all matter.

helioscope—A telescope designed for observing the sun.

lens—A piece of glass or other transparent solid with one or two curved surfaces. A lens concentrates or diffuses light rays as they pass through it. Lenses are used in optical instruments including telescopes and microscopes.

microscope—An optical instrument that uses lenses to produce magnified images of small objects.

multifaceted—Having many sides.

natural philosopher—A person who studied the nature of the physical universe before the development of modern science.

navigator—A person who plots the course of a ship or a plane.

patent—An official document that gives a person or company the exclusive right to make or sell an invention.

pendulum—A weight hung at the end of a string or rod that can swing freely under the influence of gravity.

perforated—Pierced with holes.

porous—Having many pores or tiny openings.

portrait—A drawing, painting, or photograph of a person.

prism—Clear pieces of glass that can disperse light into a spectrum.

prodigious—Wonderful, amazing.

quarantine—Isolation imposed on people or animals to try to stop the spread of disease.

rhetoric—The art of using language to influence others.

sash window—A window that slides vertically on a system of cords and balanced weights.

specimen—A sample or an individual or part used as an example for scientific examination.

spectrum—The range of colors from short wavelengths (violet) to long wavelengths (red).

survey—To measure or map the land.

tendril—A threadlike part of a plant.

thatched—Roofing made of straw.

theory—In science, an explanation of how or why a natural phenomenon occurs.

transfusion—To transfer blood from one person or animal to another.

universal joint—A mechanical connection that allows a rigid rod to "bend" in different directions. A universal joint can connect two rotating shafts.

zenith—The point in the sky directly over the observer.

Further Reading

Books

Chapman, Allan. *England's Leonardo: Robert Hooke and the Seventeenth-Century Scientific Revolution*. London, England: Institute of Physics, 2005.

Cooper, Michael. *Robert Hooke and the Rebuilding of London*. Thrupp, Stroud, England: Sutton Publishing, 2005.

Drake, Ellen Tan. *Restless Genius: Robert Hooke and His Earthly Thoughts*. New York: Oxford University Press, 1996.

Gow, Mary. *Robert Boyle: Pioneer of Experimental Chemistry*. Berkeley Heights, N.J.: Enslow Publishers, Inc., 2005.

Inwood, Stephen. *The Forgotten Genius: the Biography of Robert Hooke 1635–1703*. San Francisco. MacAdam/ Cage Publishing, 2005.

Internet Addresses

Robert Hooke (1635–1703)

http://www.ucmp.berkeley.edu/history/hooke.html

Robert Hooke.org

http://www.roberthooke.org.uk/

Robert Boyle and Robert Hooke, University College, Oxford

http://web.comlab.ox.ac.uk/oxinfo/univ-col/ boyle-hooke.html

Index